MULTICULTURAL EDUCATION SERIES

James A. Banks, *Series Editor*

Multicultural Education, Transformative Knowledge, and Action:
Historical and Contemporary Perspectives
JAMES A. BANKS, Editor

Educating Citizens in a Multicultural Society
JAMES A. BANKS

We Can't Teach What We Don't Know:
White Teachers, Multiracial Schools
GARY R. HOWARD

Reducing Prejudice and Stereotyping in Schools
WALTER STEPHAN

The Light in Their Eyes:
Creating Multicultural Learning Communities
SONIA NIETO

Race and Culture in the Classroom:
Teaching and Learning Through Multicultural Education
MARY DILG

Race and Culture in the Classroom

Teaching and Learning Through Multicultural Education

MARY DILG

FOREWORD BY JAMES A. BANKS

Teachers College, Columbia University
New York and London

Published by Teachers College Press, 1234 Amsterdam Avenue, New York, NY 10027

An earlier version of Chapter 2 appeared in *English Journal*, March 1995, volume 84, number 3, pp. 18–25. Reprinted with permission.

An earlier version of Chapter 6 appeared in *English Journal*, October 1997, volume 86, number 6, pp. 64–69. Reprinted with permission.

Library of Congress Cataloging-in-Publication Data

Dilg, Mary.
    Race and culture in the classroom : teaching and learning through
multicultural education / Mary Dilg : foreword by James A. Banks.
       p.   cm. — (Multicultural education series)
    Includes bibliographical references (p.   ) and index.
    ISBN 0-8077-3823-9 (cloth). — ISBN 0-8077-3822-0 (paper)
    1. Multicultural education—United States. 2. Race relations—
Study and teaching—United States. 3. Culture—Study and teaching—
United States. I. Title. II. Series: Multicultural education
series (New York, N.Y.)
LC1099.3.D55   1999
370.117′0973—DC21   98-55473

ISBN 0-8077-3822-0 (paper)
ISBN 0-8077-3823-9 (cloth)

Printed on acid-free paper

Manufactured in the United States of America

06 05 04 03 02 01 00 99   8 7 6 5 4 3 2 1

For Fennie Curry and Elsa Baehr:
Amid "circles and circles of sorrow," love.

CONTENTS

SERIES FOREWORD

The nation's deepening ethnic texture, interracial tension and conflict, and the increasing percentage of students who speak a first language other than English make multicultural education an imperative as we enter a new century. The 1990 Census indicated that one of every four Americans is a person of color. About one out of every three Americans will be a person of color by the turn of the century.

American classrooms are experiencing the largest influx of immigrant students since the turn of the century. More than eight million legal immigrants settled in the United States between 1981 and 1990 (U. S. Bureau of the Census, 1994). A large but undetermined number of undocumented immigrants also enter the United States each year. The influence of an increasingly ethnically diverse population on the nation's schools, colleges, and universities is and will continue to be enormous. In 50 of the nation's largest urban public school systems, African Americans, Latinos, Asian Americans, and other students of color made up 76.5 percent of the student population in 1992 (Council of the Great City Schools, 1994). In some of the nation's largest cities and metropolitan areas, such as Chicago, Los Angeles, Washington, D. C., New York, Seattle, and San Francisco, half or more of the public school students are students of color. In California, the population of students of color in the public schools has exceeded the percentage of White students since the 1988–89 school year.

Students of color will make up about 46 percent of the nation's student population by 2020 (Pallas, Natriello, & McDill, 1989). Fourteen percent of school-age youth live in homes in which English is not the first language (U. S. Bureau of the Census, 1994). Most teachers now in the classroom and in teacher education programs are likely to have students from diverse ethnic, cultural, and racial groups in their classrooms during their careers. This is true for both inner-city and suburban teachers.

An important goal of multicultural education is to improve race relations and to help all students acquire the knowledge, attitudes, and skills needed to participate in cross-cultural interactions and in personal, social, and civic action that will help make our nation more democratic and just. Multicultural education is consequently as important for middle-class White suburban students as it is for students of color who live in the inner-city. Multicultural education fosters the public good and the overarching goals of the commonwealth.

The major purpose of the *Multicultural Education Series* is to provide pre-service educators, practicing educators, graduate students, and scholars with an interrelated and comprehensive set of books that summarizes and analyzes important research, theory, and practice related to the education of ethnic, racial, cultural, and language groups in the United States and the education of mainstream students about ethnic and cultural diversity. The books in the *Series* provide research, theoretical, and practical knowledge about the behaviors and learning characteristics of students of color, language minority students, and low-income students. They also provide knowledge about ways to improve race relations in educational settings.

The definition of multicultural education in the *Handbook of Research on Multicultural Education* (Banks & Banks, 1995) is used in the *Series*: "multicultural education is a field of study designed to increase educational equity for all students that incorporates, for this purpose, content, concepts, principles, theories, and paradigms from history, the social and behavioral sciences, and particularly from ethnic studies and women studies" (p. xii). In the *Series*, as in the *Handbook*, multicultural education is considered a "metadiscipline."

The dimensions of multicultural education, developed by Banks (1995) and described in the *Handbook of Research on Multicultural Education*, provide the conceptual framework for the development of the books in the *Series*. They are: *content integration, the knowledge construction process, prejudice reduction, an equity pedagogy*, and *an empowering school culture and social structure*. To implement multicultural education effectively, teachers and administrators must attend to each of the five dimensions of multicultural education. They should use content from diverse groups when teaching concepts and skills, help students to understand how knowledge in the various disciplines is constructed, help students to develop positive intergroup attitudes and behaviors, and modify their teaching strategies so that students from different racial, cultural, and social-class groups will experience equal educational opportunities. The total environment and culture of the school must also be transformed so that students from diverse ethnic and cultural groups will experience equal status in the culture and life of the school.

Although the five dimensions of multicultural education are highly interrelated, each requires deliberate attention and focus. Each book in the series focuses on one or more of the dimensions, although each book deals with all of them to some extent because of the highly interrelated characteristics of the dimensions.

This insightful and gracefully written book by a gifted and perceptive classroom teacher epitomizes the important role of the teacher in creating culturally democratic classrooms and schools. Dilg listens carefully to the voices of her students and empowers them. She understands how the racial struggles and interactions they experience in the classroom mirror those in the larger society.

Dilg describes how teachers can model democracy by helping students to acquire knowledge about their own cultures and histories as well as knowledge about the groups to which their classmates belong. One of her important goals is to help her students become thoughtful and compassionate citizen actors in a democratic society.

Reflective accounts of their teaching by talented and perceptive teachers such as Sylvia Ashton-Warner, Herbert Kohl, Ira Shor, and Vivian Paley describe ways in which important ideas about education can become realities in classrooms. They consequently give hope and possibilities to other teachers who wish to transform their classrooms and schools. With the publication of this book, Mary Dilg joins the list of insightful teachers who inspire and encourage other teachers to change the ways they think and teach. This book will motivate and encourage teachers not just because Dilg describes her successes, but more importantly because she shares her challenges and doubts, and consequently conveys how powerful teaching is a complex and difficult but rewarding endeavor. I am confident that this incisive book will find the place on the bookshelves of caring and committed educators that it deserves.

—James A. Banks
Series Editor

REFERENCES

Banks, J. A. (1995). Multicultural education: Historical development, dimensions, and practice. In J. A. Banks & C. A. M. Banks (Eds.), *Handbook of research on multicultural education* (pp. 3–24). New York: Macmillan.

Banks, J. A., & Banks, C. A. M. (Eds.) (1995). *Handbook of research on multicultural education.* New York: Macmillan.

Council of the Great City Schools (1994). *National urban education goals: 1992–1993 indicators report.* Washington, D. C.: Author.

Pallas, A. M., Natriello, G., & McDill, E. L. (1989). The changing nature of the disadvantaged population: Current dimensions and future trends. *Educational Researcher, 18* (5), 16–22.

U.S. Bureau of the Census (1994). *Statistical abstract of the United States* (114th edition). Washington, D. C.: U. S. Government Printing Office.

ACKNOWLEDGMENTS

Readers at the *Harvard Educational Review* and *Teachers College Record* offered useful responses to earlier versions of several of these chapters. Leila Christenbury, editor of *English Journal*, honored the voices of these students by publishing the first of these essays. Dr. James Banks of the University of Washington and Brian Ellerbeck of Teachers College Press provided the most enviable continued editorial encouragement a writer could find. Lori Tate, also of Teachers College Press, provided editorial assistance and saw the book through the production process.

Friends and colleagues at the Francis W. Parker School have been generous about this work from the beginning, and have created a school in which adults as well as children can find joy in learning. Dr. Donald Monroe and his predecessors Dr. Timothy Burns and John Cotton were willing to stand behind team teaching in an era of shrinking budgets and expanding needs. Dr. Daniel Frank shared not only his wisdom about adolescents and families, but also his idea of regarding classroom discussions as texts, an idea germane to observations throughout these essays. Dr. Andrew Kaplan and Harriett Cholden have always been available for thoughtful conversations as well as critiques of the work as it came into being. My students, in their willingness to share their questions and concerns, have shown me what I needed to learn. My friend and teaching partner Robert Merrick, Chairman of the History Department and virtuosic teacher, made these essays possible. From talks on John Hope Franklin to Ludwig Wittgenstein, from conversations on the meanings of adolescent cross-cultural discussions to ongoing collaboration in the development of curriculum and pedagogy for cross-cultural studies, his ideas and support lie behind every page. Any errors are my own.

My parents provided the bi-regional upbringing which gave birth to this work. My husband, Russ, and children, Aynsley and Justin, lovers of ideas all, have believed in every stage of this work and in what it's about.

Race and Culture in the Classroom

Teaching and Learning Through
Multicultural Education

LISTENING TO THE STUDENTS

In 1960, psychiatrist and educator Robert Coles met a young Black girl named Ruby Bridges as she integrated the New Orleans public schools. Day after day, Ruby walked to her elementary school surrounded by federal marshals as angry White adults spit at her and called her names. But she did not falter, and later she explained that she had prayed for those who had tormented her. Ruby Bridges was six years old. Intrigued by her strength, Dr. Coles spent hours interviewing her, and her story would grace many of the pages he would write about that era (1964, 1986, 1993, 1995, 1997).

Several aspects of those moments involving Robert Coles, Ruby Bridges, and other children like her continue to haunt me as I work with adolescents grappling with issues of race and culture in the 1990s: significant social change was taking place because of children, in schools. The children were willing to engage themselves in crucial social issues in ways in which many adults were not. The children were simultaneously victims of their nation's social divides and bearers of the idealism and moral courage necessary to address those divides. And, as Coles himself has so eloquently described, this young Black girl from Louisiana had much to teach the Harvard professor.

Though much has changed since Ruby took her walk to school, students today are still surrounded by challenges emanating from the multicultural nature of their nation and their schools. Schools remain the sites of social challenges and social change. Students today continue to be the victims of racial and cultural divisiveness, yet they are also among those most eager to understand and to close the gaps that divide us.

For us as educators, addressing the racial and cultural issues that have emerged in schools today means rethinking some of our most basic assumptions about teaching and learning—what we teach and how. And working with these issues is never easy—for students or for teachers. But as those moments between Ruby Bridges and Robert Coles can also remind us, students themselves have much to teach us as together we address the challenges before us.

Aided by images in popular culture, most of us are accustomed to the role of teacher as speaker. But in the essays that follow, the teacher is mostly a listener. The teacher, in fact, has become mostly a student. This has often meant the teacher is viewed not as authoritarian, the central figure, or the speaker, but as the listener, the observer, the recorder. As Coles's own mentor Anna Freud

1

once remarked, "Let us try to learn from children all they have to tell us" (Coles, 1986, p. 15). That is the process represented in these essays.

Thus although these essays are filled with lessons, in most instances they are lessons the students have taught the teacher. As these students have taught me, so may they now teach others.

POINTS OF VIEW

All of these essays represent the point of view of an English teacher—not a sociologist, anthropologist, psychologist, or formal educational researcher. They reflect a teacher attempting to understand and address significant challenges emerging in our schools and classrooms today as students from multiple cultures live and learn together—however raggedly, however painfully, however full of hope. The essays have come into being through years of observing and of taking notes on the conversations of adolescents as they engage in discussions about issues of race and culture—in classrooms, in hallways, or in public forums.

The school where these conversations have taken place is a private progressive high school in a major metropolitan area. The school's philosophy is grounded in the progressive principles of John Dewey and Francis Parker. The school serves students from a wide range of socioeconomic backgrounds. Of approximately 300 students, roughly 18 percent are students of color. Pseudonyms are used in these essays, and identifying details have been changed to protect the privacy of individuals. Racial or cultural identities, where provided, are used not to construct artificial divisions among the students, but because those identities are often a significant factor in observations, discussions, or group dynamics related to racial or cultural issues.

As someone who has worked with adolescents in urban public and private schools for over 20 years, I well appreciate the degree to which teaching conditions and the needs of students vary from school to school. But racial and cultural tensions have emerged in schools across the nation. The essays provided here have grown out of working closely with adolescents attempting to come to terms with those issues as they surround them every day—in their schools or in their communities. What the essays reveal of that process should be of use in a wide variety of settings.

Specific courses described in these essays have been designed with my own students in mind, and materials used in those courses range from films and newspaper articles to texts perhaps more frequently associated with university teaching. But working with issues of race and culture—studying them, having conversations about them—may take place as readily or easily (or with as much difficulty) through the use of texts taken from anthologies, or magazines, or newspapers, as it can through the use of the specific materials noted here—*as long as the texts and materials represent perspectives from multiple cultures.* In schools where existing teaching materials are grounded exclusively in the perspectives of those from the dominant culture, teachers must be willing to lobby for resources to expand the range of materials available or to supplement available materials with others they bring in on their own. It is my belief that effective teaching or learning about these issues can take place *only* through studying the perspectives of those from multiple cultures, especially the perspectives of people of color. Further, although one of the courses described here is an interdisciplinary course with the more unusual staffing arrangement of team teaching, others are English courses I have taught alone, not as part of a team.

Because concepts central to a discussion of racial or cultural issues or multicultural education continue to be ever changing and controversial, the meanings of several words used throughout the essays warrant clarification. The first are *race, ethnicity*, and *culture*. Although some contend that race is a purely artificial construct or even an illusion, it continues to occupy discussions of the past and the present. One useful framework for the term as it appears in these essays is offered by the authors of *Race, Class, and Gender*: "Race is a social-historical-political concept [Omi & Winant, 1986]. Societies construct race, and racial meanings constantly change because different groups contest prevailing racial definitions that empower some groups at the expense of others" (Andersen & Collins, 1995, p. 61). *Ethnicity* can refer simply to a minority group within a larger community, or, according to sociologist Margaret Andersen, to a "group that shares . . . some common cultural heritage . . . " ("Ethnicity," 1997, p. 177). According to Andersen and Collins, the 1990 census forms listed five racial categories—White; Black or African American; Asian or Pacific Islander; American Indian, Eskimo, or Aleut; and "other"—and two ethnicities, Hispanic or non-Hispanic. However, the meanings of race and ethnicity overlap because, according to Andersen and Collins, " . . . Hispanics may be of any race . . . " (Andersen & Collins, 1995, p. 61).

Additionally, when students discuss the issues, they slide from a focus that might technically be associated with race to a focus that might technically be associated with ethnicity, without stopping to distinguish between them. A teacher can offer students various meanings of each term. But actual student conversations yield moments in which the concepts are blended or overlapping. My goal in these essays is to render students' conversations as accurately as possible for the reader. Thus although distinctions exist between the concepts of race and ethnicity, given that the concepts also overlap and that students may blur the distinctions between them in conversations, in these essays I have not distinguished between the two. The term *culture* is used here to refer to the history, language, customs, values, traditions, or worldview of a particular group at a particular time.

Most of the issues adolescents confront in these essays are associated in some way with one of two concepts—race or culture. Those issues might include, for example, racism, prejudice, separatism, affirmative action, immigration, bilingual education, or hate crimes. Or the issues might emerge from any aspect of the converging or diverging histories, customs, or values surrounding the students.

"Issues of race and culture" is used as an inclusive phrase to designate any one or more of these types of issues that affect students or that become the subject of inquiry in their discussions. "Issues of Race and Culture" is the title of one of the school's elective courses, which produced much of the information in the essays.

Multicultural education is the other term that must be clarified. Few educational movements have excited such controversy. Individuals and groups ascribe a host of contradictory meanings to the term to fit their own needs or arguments—so much so that articles may now include a whole list of meanings associated with the term. In these essays the term is associated with the following assumptions.

1. A central goal of the school should be to create an atmosphere in which teachers, students, and families can work and play together with knowledge of and respect for each other.
2. Teachers should recognize the significant difficulties that students and families face in coming together and creating a multicultural community, and they should be committed to assisting them in that process.
3. Teachers should make use of a multicultural sensitivity in shaping curriculum and pedagogy; they should have some working knowledge of the histories, cultures, and learning styles of their students and draw on that knowledge in ways that will provide a meaningful learning experience for each of their students as well as for their classes as a whole.
4. Multicultural education makes significant demands on teachers and on students and is in no way associated with a diminution in intellectual rigor.
5. Multicultural education as used in these essays is associated with support for individual, group, and community needs, even though at times those needs may be competing.
6. Multicultural education is associated with inclusion, not balkanization, breadth rather than narrowness, wholeness rather than fragmentation.
7. A key assumption is that multicultural education can provide the basis for a fuller, more satisfying life in this multicultural nation.

THE LESSONS

The first essay, "The Other Day at School: Cross-cultural Challenges in a High School Community," had its origin in a morning assembly which unexpectedly triggered a racial incident and released pent-up and simmering emotions. Responding to the obvious confusion and distress of the students, administrators set up a series of discussion groups on racial and cultural dynamics in the school, with someone in each group assigned to take notes.

What those discussions revealed, in the students' own words, was a broad range of racial and cultural challenges that surrounded them every day, in classes, in hallways, and during their leisure time. Perhaps not surprisingly, the concerns articulated by the students consistently reflected similar unresolved concerns voiced throughout adult communities in this country and by some of our most astute thinkers and writers on these issues. That the students were articulating these same concerns during their adolescence in an educational setting, and making thoughtful suggestions for addressing them, provided an extraordinary opportunity for significant teaching and learning. The moment and its follow-up discussions provided an invitation to teachers and administrators to devise curricular and extracurricular means for addressing the students' questions and concerns. It was the essence of what some would call the "teachable moment."

The students were telling us candidly, broadly, what they needed to know. Their articulation of specific concerns could be used as a blueprint for responsive educational planning. With such planning emerging in part from the students' own observations and suggestions, a rare opportunity existed for students, faculty members, and administrators to work together in a way that could move the school closer to exemplifying its own historical and philosophical ideals. The essay that grew out of these circumstances suggests that such unexpected moments of racial or cultural tension can thus become the source of much learning—for adults and for students in the school community.

Although the incident that resulted in the first essay emerged in the relatively open arena of a schoolwide activity, equally intense racial and cultural dynamics may be triggered in classrooms as groups of students from multiple cultures explore texts related to racial or cultural issues. The next series of essays explores some of those dynamics as they shape and impinge upon classroom teaching and learning.

"The Opening of the American Mind: Challenges in the Cross-cultural Teaching of Literature" was born of the confluence of several contrary patterns of thought about multicultural education. On the national level, major newspapers were regularly carrying stories in which critics of multiculturalism decried what they saw as an essential challenge to rigorous thinking, and a drift away from a crucial grounding in the canon associated with Western civilization, as schools included courses and texts focusing on nondominant cultures. Although many of these arguments focused on highly politicized incidents and activities at the university level—including statements by Professor Leonard Jeffries at City College of New York, a general growing interest in Afrocentrism, and pressures linking alumni funding to undergraduate curriculum at Yale University—arguments by authors such as Allan Bloom, Lynne Cheney, and Dinesh D'Souza were directly relevant to the teaching I was engaged in at the secondary level.

But based on my own experiences with students, many of the arguments opposing multicultural education did not cohere. On one hand, the histories and texts of non-dominant populations are as complex and provocative and descriptive of the human experience as those texts and courses that have won approval for their focus on Western civilization. As someone who has spent all her professional life with great literature, for example, I know that the works of Toni Morrison must be accorded a place beside those of John Milton and Leo Tolstoy and James Joyce. The routes toward knowledge are various, and always incomplete. We pick and choose our competencies no matter the route or requirements; developing certain strengths always means neglecting others.

Additionally, the words and actions of students around me daily revealed a need for them to learn about each other's histories and cultures in order to develop a more cohesive understanding of each other and to build a more satisfactory community.

I had also witnessed, innumerable times, the powerful effects that works by writers of color could have on students. For students of color, the texts often succeeded in making literature meaningful, in giving them back their history or in explaining that history to their classmates, in helping them feel less alone in their life experiences, in making them feel part of the educational and dialogical process in classrooms, or in giving them role models or directions for their future. For many White students, these works opened up new worlds and new perspectives.

Based on the artistry of the works, the needs of the students, and the effect of the works on students, I knew that I must offer these texts, this focus, in my classes. Repeatedly, however, in doing so, I left class feeling uneasy. What was I doing wrong? Why was my decision to include these texts not resulting in a deeper sense of rightness and satisfaction? The answer lay in the complexity at the heart of multicultural education. I did not know enough to handle these works well in a classroom.

To approach effectively these works of literature, the issues they focus on, and the dynamics they may trigger among students requires not only a grounding in the literature of multiple cultures, but a knowledge of history, political science, sociology, anthropology, psychology, group dynamics, and conflict management—a breadth and depth of background most of us in my generation lack, even after we have gone through well-respected undergraduate and graduate programs in liberal arts.

Working with texts in multicultural groups of students stirs up passions and emotions difficult to work with and to guide constructively. The same closeness students feel with this material because of the way in which it confronts real issues in their lives makes the material very challenging to work with in class.

Students' racial or cultural identities affect what they bring to the texts and how they are affected by them. Their engagement with the texts and in discussions will also be powerfully affected by where they are in developing their own identities, where they are in relation to their own history and culture, and how they feel about the histories and cultures of others. Additionally, the process of analyzing the students' own cultures or cultural histories as part of examining specific issues can tax both individuals and the group. Through natural and powerful identifications with their own cultures, students may feel that they, their families, their cultures, their histories, or their classmates have become the subject of study by the class. At times this can produce excitement and pride, but the process can also produce tense and uncomfortable moments.

Discussions of texts focusing directly on issues of race or culture are unpredictable and volatile. For the teacher, it is impossible to know what type of remark will emerge in a seminar, especially from adolescents who are still developing skills in public discourse and sensitivity to each other across racial and cultural lines. It is also difficult to know the best moment to intervene. Sometimes, responses to difficult moments or statements are most effective when they come from the students. At other times, the direction or tenor of a discussion necessitates prompt intervention—a reminder of discussion guidelines, clarification of a point, redirection of the conversation, or support for individuals or the group—on the part of the teacher. Many times, the best course of action in a difficult moment may not be clear until later, after reflecting on the moment and the options for addressing it. And there are some moments in these conversations that are going to be hurtful no matter what other students or a teacher can do—reality in these matters is, in and of itself, often painful.

Arcing over the complexities involved in working with these texts and issues was the ongoing conviction that we simply must address these issues with students for the sake of building more harmonious communities—in school and beyond.

Knowing firsthand the complexities inherent in multicultural education, I was frustrated both with the casting of the movement as "dumb" by its critics and by a growing sense of the inadequacy of my own knowledge and skills to deal effectively with the challenges of multicultural teaching and learning emerging directly in front of me.

Thus it was that I began to study the dynamics around me in a variety of my own courses as students encountered, studied, or discussed issues of race or culture. I needed to understand why certain types of moments were occurring and how to avoid or better address other moments. I needed to observe students, listen to them, and try to understand what they were saying.

This was made dramatically clear one morning when an explosive discussion occurred unexpectedly in a class on twentieth-century fiction. That discussion is described and analyzed in "Reading the Text of the Talking: A Novel Approach to Understanding the Impact of Cultural Divisiveness on Adolescents." In approaching a work of contemporary fiction about the Holocaust, my students' interests and passions uncovered chasms among us that I was paralyzed to know how to address. What gave rise to the writing of the essay was my profound sense of failure at the end of that class. Only after exploring aspects of the discussion over a period of months, and eventually writing the essay, was I able to understand the discussion fully enough to learn from it and therefore to be able to carry its lessons into future classes.

In addition to the discoveries I was making in English courses as students encountered literature by writers of color, there was the work that was unfolding simultaneously in the course Issues of Race and Culture. In 1991, a history department colleague and I had developed a team-taught, interdisciplinary elective course for juniors and seniors which would directly explore issues of race and culture through the work of scholars and artists from multiple cultures.

In addition to what the course could provide for students, it afforded the two of us an opportunity to learn more about multicultural education. Three times a week, adolescents from multiple cultures came before us to confront significant racial and cultural issues together. The interdisciplinary nature of the course meant that students would be working with multiple types of authorities and approaches to the issues, and this allowed us to begin to understand how students approached and were affected by a variety of texts and materials. The fact that it was team taught allowed one of us to observe the process of teaching and learning about these issues while the other was teaching. It also yielded dialogues between the two of us over a period of years through which we were able to note and analyze dynamics unfolding throughout the course.

These observations and dialogues allowed us to begin to understand multicultural education as it involves adolescents working directly with issues of race and culture. We learned about the effects of the order in which various cultures or materials were considered relative to the racial or cultural makeup of the class. We learned about the probable effects of some texts on students and their discussions and the unpredictability of the ways other texts would affect them. We learned about the sometimes unwanted effects of employing progressive or experiential teaching methods for working with already provocative texts. We learned about the impact of individual and group identities and histories on the study of these issues. We came to identify factors that make learning about these issues from multiple viewpoints at once so important and so difficult. We began to identify and understand a cycle of emotions that defines the ebb and flow of the feelings of students—and teachers—as they work with these issues together. We came to understand what this kind of teaching expects and demands of students and teachers. In short, we came to know more about why multicultural education is so hard—for students and for teachers. Some of these lessons are described in the essays "What We Learned in School Today: Teaching Issues of Race and Culture" and "Idealization, Disillusionment, and Reparation in Teaching about Race and Culture."

The last essay, "Why I Am a Multiculturalist: The Power of Stories Told and Untold," emerged from the process and the premise that originally raised questions about multicultural education in my mind—the teaching of literature and the conviction that it is a good and necessary thing that our reading lists and the focus of our courses be grounded in a base of multiple cultures. Ultimately, the last essay suggests, we all stand to gain from hearing each other's stories.

TOWARD MULTICULTURAL EDUCATION

As I write this, demographic studies tell us that our student population is becoming more diverse, and our faculties are becoming more monocultural (Cotton, 1993). Our schools are re-segregating (Applebome, 1997), and thus our students will have less chance of working together and learning about each other across racial and cultural lines. Yet hosts of schools and classes still bring together, every day, students from multiple cultures who have little understanding of each other. And whether in schools that serve populations of over 90 percent students of color, or in schools that afford White students little opportunity to know and work with students of color, studies continue to show that writers of color have gained little prominent entry into secondary school reading lists (Applebome, 1995). What all these studies suggest is that significant challenges lie before us in creating schools in which teachers, students, and families can interact across racial and cultural lines in ways that foster meaningful learning and create the foundations for more cohesive communities.

In the summer of 1996, I was studying in Australia and experienced being an outsider firsthand. As a result, I wanted to come home. In fact, I did return home prematurely, broken in part by an overwhelming sense of alienation. Even in a country where the majority was, like me, White and English speaking, I could not tolerate the effects of alienation. I did not know or understand enough about the culture around me to feel comfortable. But in our multicultural classes, our students *are* home, and if they do not feel included, if they do not feel part of the focus of their texts or their courses or the process of learning, most of them have neither the power nor the choice to place themselves in a more comfortable or inclusive setting.

So it falls to all of us who care about these children to make sure that all our classes are home to each student and that we provide our students with the knowledge and skills necessary for them to live better and fuller lives in this multicultural nation. I believe a multicultural curriculum and an understanding of the complexities inherent in the pedagogy of multiculturalism can help us begin to realize that goal.

Despite the challenges such teaching and learning put before us, and despite our lack of readiness to meet those demands, the reality of our students' lives and the nature of this nation demand that we embrace a multicultural foundation for the education of our teachers, for the designing of our courses, and for the breadth of our pedagogy. To do so is not to sacrifice "great" voices for "lesser" ones, but rather to enlarge the circle of the thinkers before us, to invite contemporary thinkers to join more traditional thinkers, to invite less familiar voices to join those who have already gained prominence. We will all be the richer for our enlarged circle of thought. Nor does this choice threaten to divide us, in a dangerous manner, into subcultures. It is rather a recognition of each other, and an invitation to move forward together. It may be one of the least "dumb" gestures we have ever made.

A LEGACY OF TEACHING

Lastly, there is a particular spirit surrounding these essays that comes from a long line of educators who have cared deeply about children. Imagine, if you will, a circle of folks gathered around an old wooden table at Hull House on a wintry Chicago afternoon. Conversing this afternoon are Jane Addams, John Dewey, Francis Parker, Anna Freud, Robert Coles, and Vivian Paley. What these thinkers have in common is an abiding concern for children in a chaotic world that can easily use and abuse them. They care about the dignity and inner life of the child. They care about a child's growing and changing sense of identity and how hard it is, sometimes, to be engaged in that process of creating a self. They care that children know and connect with others in ways that can better the children's own lives and our neighborhoods and communities. They recognize that children suffer and are keenly aware of the suffering all around them. They know that children are wise and that children "have much to teach us" (Paley, 1989, p. 142), if only we will listen.

It is the values of those educators and writers that inform my wanting to listen carefully to my students over the years. A supportive and intellectually engaging community in the school where I teach has made that possible.

CHAPTER 1

THE OTHER DAY AT SCHOOL

Cross-cultural Challenges in a High School Community

On a recent spring morning, the students of an urban, private progressive high school filed into the auditorium for what promised to be an entertaining half-hour. The Video Club, comprised mostly of White students, would be screening prize-winning student videos. The lights dimmed, and a series of fast-paced videos from a generation of filmmakers raised on MTV jittered across the over-sized screen. Then the screen went blank. While Video Club members changed the videocassette during a brief intermission, popular music blared over the sound system, and on stage, several young Black males began to dance, bending and dipping their bodies to the rhythms of the music. Students applauded and laughed. The dancing ended, the audience viewed the remaining videos, and the program was brought to a close.

A few minutes later, in the same auditorium, the weekly meeting of the student government was called to order. Within minutes suppressed racial and cultural tensions in the group erupted. In a lightning series of moments, several young Black women spoke up. "We were deeply offended by the guys dancing on stage. It was like the minstrel shows, Black men dancing for the entertainment of Whites." Several other young Black women were quick to respond, equally offended—*but by what they had just heard.* "Those moments were not about race, they were about being human—the audience was being unkind to fellow students." The young women who had raised the issue charged their respondents with knowing nothing of their heritage. Several of the young women's passions intensified, but they were prevented from harming each other by a young White male who placed himself between them.

Once the intensity of the initial responses subsided, the assembly dispersed. Students went their separate ways, cried, and formed hushed circles in unusually quiet halls. Many sought advice from teachers as to how this could happen in an otherwise vibrant and purposeful one-hundred-year-old school historically devoted to humanitarian goals. Several members of the Video Club broke down and sobbed. The young Black women, angry, confused, and tear-stained, sought refuge with friends.

The exact reasons for such a swift, vocal, and emotionally intense reaction to what had occurred as the program unfolded that morning remain unclear. But beyond the larger issues at work in a multicultural community explored in this essay, several factors may have coalesced to create the students' responses.

Although the incident occurred in the high school division of the school, the school itself is a K–12 school. Except for students who had transferred into the school during the middle or high school years, the majority gathered that morning had known each other for more than 10 years. The student body is also predominantly White, and many of the students of color are among those who join the community during middle and high school years.

Beyond their familiarity—and therefore, somewhat, their predictability—with each other, over the years, many students come to idealize the school and its community. Somehow, they maintain, the community of the school should be free of the racial and cultural divisions beyond its doors. Their idealism feeds an ongoing belief in the possibility of building and maintaining a more ideal community than the ones that surround them outside of the school.

Additionally, developmentally, as students leave the relatively less racially and ethnically conscious years of childhood, they enter into a period in which issues of identity become paramount. For many, that includes an exploration of their racial or cultural identity, as well as histories and values related to that identity. Moments or interactions that may have passed unnoticed or might not have even occurred when the students were younger, during the high school years, may engender passionate and brooding responses that are mystifying at times, even to the students themselves.

Last, the philosophy of the school is defined by several distinct educational and psychological values that may indirectly have contributed to such a public and vocal response. The students know throughout their years of schooling that theirs is a "progressive" school. The motto above the stage in the very room in which this outburst occurred reads: "A school should be a model home, a complete community, an embryonic democracy." In the tradition of John Dewey and Colonel Francis Parker, the school values—in teaching and in learning—personal responsibility, democratic processes, student voices, and student participation in decision making, and it places a high value on the "social motive" (Stone, 1976, p. 335) and community-mindedness.

It is also a community that values an open and analytic approach to problems. Students are encouraged to be critical thinkers and to act on their beliefs for the good of the community; to examine their own lives and the world around them in a manner at once sympathetic and analytical; and to raise questions about moments, interactions, or choices that trouble them. Although they may possess both idealism and cynicism, they also, for the most part, know that the adults around them will take seriously their observations and their concerns and be responsive in ways that can matter.

In this particular moment, some students' responses grew out of their relationship not only to their school community, but also to their own developing racial identities and an awareness of their racial histories. They experienced the Black males dancing on stage for a predominantly White audience as a reminder of a bleak and exploitative period in Black-American history. They expressed their concerns openly and vehemently in a forum designed to allow students to air their grievances and to exercise their budding skills in engaging in democratic processes. The outward expression of criticism of some members of the community on the part of several Black students, however, was experienced by other students as a shattering suggestion that the community that many had thought of as harmonious and united was not. The combination of these factors meant that the tensions that had originated among a small cluster of students rapidly rippled outward to affect an increasingly larger number of students: White students who experienced the incident as a disturbing intrusion of tensions of which they were unaware, and students of color who were considerably less sanguine about the "ideal" nature of the school community. This discrepancy between the students' yearning for a more ideal community—on the part of both students of color and White students—and the reality unfolding in front of them proved insupportable. In the face of that awareness, they took public stands to make their disillusionment and their confusion known. A week later, the student body met in small discussion groups to look at the incident and explore its meanings for the community.

WINDOW ON A HIGH SCHOOL COMMUNITY

What those discussions revealed, in a unique window on a high school community, is the following: woven throughout the larger academic and social life of the school is a series of dynamics growing out of the multicultural nature of the school community. Those dynamics pose formidable challenges to the students in ways that make it difficult for them to form a fully cohesive community. Evidence shows that those same challenges lie at the heart of the larger American society struggling with its multicultural nature. If our historical vision of ourselves as a multicultural society is to be sustainable, if we are to hope for more cohesive communities in the future, we need to address directly the challenges to those goals, in the youthful communities that are our schools.

The discussions following the original incident suggest that our students are caught in a nexus of racial and cultural dilemmas emanating from individual, group, and community dynamics, as well as from history itself. They have gained neither the experience nor the insights to avoid moments of cultural tension or to fully understand them once they occur. They know it. But they do not know the way out. And they are looking to us for help.

This chapter examines the racial and cultural challenges facing these students as expressed by the students in the discussions following the incident. It places the challenges in the context of the larger society. And it offers suggestions, from the students themselves, for addressing the challenges. The discussions following the incident involved the full high school student body of approximately 280 students, 15% of whom were students of color. Each discussion group consisted of 20 to 25 students and one or more faculty members. Although conclusions drawn throughout the article are based, except where noted, on students' own perceptions, they are based on individual voices from a wide variety of students. Thus while the individual remarks taken together form an image of a contemporary high school community, we cannot assume any one remark represents the opinion of the whole community.

As those of us who work with students know, it is often our students who are the best teachers. As they reflect on their community in the wake of this incident, these students have much to tell us. And we all have much to gain if we can respond to what they are saying.

The Making of an Incident

Incidents such as the one that occurred that spring morning emerge from a series of factors peculiar to our times and laid down in the childhoods of these students—in their society, homes, neighborhoods, and schools.

The society in which these students has matured is one in which, Cornel West has suggested, "race matters" (1993). Studs Terkel has referred to race as the "American obsession" (1992). Novelist Charles Johnson calls the 1990s the "most intensely race-conscious decade we've had in the century" (Terkel, 1992, p. 217).

The racial and cultural consciousness that surrounds the students is laced with uneasiness and disquiet. The optimism at the heart of the Civil Rights movement has given way to false assumptions about its real gains for some, and to cynicism or despair for others. And racial and cultural tensions have increased. Historian John Hope Franklin says he is "astounded at the amount of rancor. . . . The feelings that once were covert because people were ashamed of them are now expressed overtly" (Terkel, 1992, p. 5).

We are a people increasingly divided. During the 1980s, "the races have drifted apart in so many ways, have fallen out," says Douglas Massey, a professor of sociology at the University of Chicago. . . . "As public citizens, we do nothing about it. As public institutions refuse to deal with it, individuals are forced to cope. They try to put more distance between themselves and the others" (Terkel, 1992, pp. 14, 96). And some observers, such as Derrick Bell, a professor of law at New York University Law School and author of *Faces at the Bottom of the Well*, have few hopes that that trend can be reversed (1992).

In the midst of this cultural milieu, these students are regularly traversing two worlds: the largely segregated worlds of their lives outside school, and the multicultural community of their school. As Andrew Hacker has noted in *Two Nations*, even though we are a genuinely heterogeneous nation, we are still essentially a segregated society (1992). Integration simply has not taken place on a wide scale. Most of these students file into school each morning from essentially culturally homogeneous situations in their homes, neighborhoods, and religious and social experiences. The result is that most of the students come into school lacking a knowledge of those with dissimilar cultural backgrounds, lacking the experience of interacting across cultural lines, and lacking fully workable role models for doing so.

In certain ways their previous schooling has not helped. For some students, years of biased curricula have meant that they have been given little or no opportunity to learn about people of color and their histories, arts, or contributions to the national experience. Thus their schooling has not been able to compensate for lack of cross-cultural education and experience in the home or neighborhood.

Many of today's schools, however, are complex multicultural communities reflecting the unresolved issues of the larger culture. They reflect the heightened consciousness about race and culture. They reflect the growing suspicion and uneasiness among cultural groups which has deepened nationally in the last decade. They reflect the fact that we do not know each other or each other's backgrounds. They reflect the need to know on the part of students long severed from their essential histories. They reflect the fact that we have learned neither how to speak with each other nor how to work together in a fully satisfactory manner. Unlike schools at the turn of the century, which, in Dewey's thinking, provided a unifying experience for children from different groups (1944), today's schools are often the arena in which differences are played out. And arching over these pressures that divide us, they reflect the need in all of us to be known and to belong.

Thus once students walk through the doors of the school each morning, they are expected to create a fully cohesive multicultural community. But their experiences so far in their public and private spheres have left them unprepared for the cultural mix that is the school community. Most have learned de facto segregation at home but are expected to integrate at school. They have been able to learn little of each other, but they are expected to communicate and interact in ways that demand such knowledge. If, in addition, students have had negative personal experiences across cultural lines, they must overcome the effects of those experiences. And in the face of these challenges, they are uncertain about their role models for accomplishing these tasks. As a result, our students are often doing the best they can, with little practical help from the adults around them who are responsible for structuring their lives.

Thus the pressures that draw these students together and the pressures that divide them produce a simmering tension which can be stored up only for so long. The stage is always set for an incident.

Living With History

One of the primary challenges facing these students is knowing and coming to terms with history—their own and each other's. One of the reasons the original incident was so charged was that for some students it evoked degrading images from the days of slavery. What this provoked in students was a host of responses reflecting the role of history in their daily lives. These are students for whom history lives. It matters, it perplexes. Many of these students have discovered they were deprived of knowing fully their own and each other's histories. The effect of this is both the desire to know those histories and also, out of not knowing, to stumble blindly into difficult social and interpersonal situations.

To listen to these students is to know a whole series of ways in which history for them is a lively force. For some it is a tool for understanding. For others it imprisons, victimizes, and isolates. For still others it is an excuse to avoid what is unfolding around them or to push people away.

Critics of multicultural education suggest that national unity is best served by emphasizing the shared "American" history, and that to teach distinct cultural histories produces a dangerous balkanization. Such a notion, however, suggests a lack of understanding of dynamics among many of today's students. The way in which our national history has traditionally been described has not reflected a balanced approach to our past. As a result, many students presently have an incomplete, or in some cases, inaccurate, sense of history. Written from the standpoint of the victors in cultural confrontations over the years, it has given an inaccurate reading of the interaction of these groups and short shrift to the histories of specific cultural groups. This means that to a degree many students have been severed from their historical roots. Thus they are left not knowing crucial aspects of their past and therefore of themselves and each other. This directly affects all the students' daily functioning as members of a multicultural community.

For reasons of filling in their own histories and better understanding the lives of those around them, many of these students are clamoring for a more accurate rendering of history. As one White student in the follow-up discussions said, "We don't know enough about each other's heritage." "There should be a class that teaches us about formative events for races and cultures," said another. And as one Black student explained, "I learn the history of the majority. I'd like to have curriculum reflect my experiences."

This request has implications beyond issues of academics and curriculum, since the students' relationships to history are also connected to their ability to build and maintain community relatedness. Without understanding each other's histories, they are more prone to be unable to communicate effectively or comfortably with each other and to slide into insensitive thinking or acting that is based on error or stereotype, and which thus has a negative social impact.

For many of these students, history also perplexes. Lacking a full context for historically related thinking and behavior, some students lack the ability to understand why history carries such weight and passion in other students' lives. Said one White student about several Black students' reactions after the incident, "I don't understand why people reflect on the painful history of their people in their dealings *now*."

Many of these students are also attempting to understand how to live with the past. For some students, particular facts of history or the reality that for years many of those facts have been kept relatively quiet in their education has produced a type of historical anger or delayed historical response—that is, an intense emotional response to their own racial or cultural history. Many students are also responding to pain associated with the oppression of their ancestors. For many of these students, it is essential to protect their idea of the past, to wrap their arms around it metaphorically and hold onto it. Thus there emerges a broad sensitivity to a wide range of reactions to specific aspects of history. Said one Black student after the original incident, "It was an attack on my heritage." One Jewish student, in drawing a parallel between responses to this racial incident and responses to Jewish history, felt frustrated that "some people belittle historical struggles such as the Holocaust."

Another result of living with the past, however, is that students far removed from the source of historical anguish may be blamed for events of the past, and this has the potential of driving a wedge between students. In each of these observations, White students express resentment over being blamed for a past they did not create: "When you said, 'I oppressed you,' that offended me." "I feel like I'm being blamed for more than 100 years of racism." "I am a victim of America's past. I am not a victim of racism, but I am its prisoner. I have to walk on eggshells because of slavery."

Thus these students are beset with the challenges emanating from their relationship to history. At times, they stumble into destructive interactions as a result of not understanding history. Many of them seek to know more about their own and each other's histories. But the degree to which they know history is also the degree to which they may be burdened by it. Because to know history is, potentially, to set in motion the response to history. Knowing more about their histories can help these students build community through fostering a greater understanding of each other. But it can also provide the information that generates anger, accusation, guilt, confusion, and resentment, all of which potentially divide a community.

Dynamics Across the Community

Another cluster of challenges facing these students has its locus in their fundamental daily interactions. What their observations reveal is that most of these
students simply do not know quite how to be together in a multicultural community. They are groping for an understanding about each other's identities and
cultures, about how to talk to and interact with each other, about how to understand basic issues of race and culture, and about how to assess incidents that
emerge among them.

Repeatedly in the wake of the original incident, students have told us they
do not "know" each other. Many of these students are experiencing the effects
not only of years of not having a balanced approach to education—of our
schools teaching particular voices and perspectives at the expense of others—but
of the divisions in our communities that have tended to separate one race or
culture from another. As a result, most do not know enough about each other
or each other's cultures to interact in ways that promote harmony and avoid
insensitivity, conflict, and dissension. So the students are left without enough
knowledge to work and play together comfortably. They tell us, "We can't know
the experiences of other people, so we can't explain their behavior." "We have
no background. We're not taught how to deal with racial issues." Said one
White student whose words were echoed by many, "I was shocked Blacks felt
apart in this society." In the words of another, "I needed to be told [about how
Black students were feeling]. I hadn't a clue that these problems were there."

Many of the students agree that being together harmoniously depends on
open communication, in being candid with each other about issues of race and
culture. As one White student noted, "Communication is the key to understanding." Or as one Black student explained, "We need to be open and specific
about racism and what hurts."

But communication about these issues is difficult and far from automatic.
First, students understand that our very language presents challenges, especially
in matters of cultural identity. The language used in self-identification of population groups is always in flux, and that complicates communication. Students
are uncertain how to address each other. Said one White student, "Should we
call [students of color] 'Blacks'? 'Afro-Americans'? 'Hispanics'?"

The students are also struggling to understand basic concepts related to
race. They do not as yet have a working vocabulary that enables them to understand racial or cultural dynamics. Many of the students' questions and observations in the discussions focused on trying to understand the concept of racism
itself. "What is racism?" they ask. Other students attempt to answer the question: "Racism is something that hurts someone." "Racism is not an incident, it's
an attitude." "If someone's offended, it is racism." "If someone violates who
you are, then it's racism."

Although working definitions of racially related concepts are easy enough to address, what becomes readily apparent is that the students' questions about language quickly become questions that can be addressed only by addressing larger issues of history, power, politics, and interpersonal and intergroup dynamics: "We need to know why something is racist." "Where does the hatred come from? Why does it exist?" "How can we handle the consequences [of racism] even if it's unintentional?"

Beyond uncertainty about language and concepts, students are also uncomfortable actually discussing these issues. As one White student suggested, many students are uneasy admitting that there is racism in the community, and they fear that they or their comments will be construed as racist. As another White student explained, "The potential for misunderstanding is high. Discriminatory remarks may be made unintentionally."

Even humor, often reliable for relieving tensions, is complicated by issues of race and culture. As these students have discovered, humor can have high stakes. Many students are aware that there is a very fine line between jesting that underscores camaraderie and jesting that alienates, and they are unsure of the ground rules. As the following remarks indicate, students are struggling with the role of humor as it relates to race or culture. As several White students observed, "People within a racial group can make fun of each other. Blacks can call each other 'nigger,' but Whites can't. Jews can make fun of each other." "I get offended when I see Blacks make fun of each other." One Black student said, "I can make jokes about myself, but others don't feel comfortable joking back."

Thus communication can often be unsatisfactory, and this means students may not want to discuss these issues. This creates tension. One White student explained, "Constricted conversations create a pressure cooker. We're afraid of doing what's wrong." Another said, "We're daily walking a tightrope trying to keep everybody happy, to not offend, but [what we communicate] may not be what we're really thinking." As their comments suggest, these students feel that developing trust requires open communication, but open communication requires trust. "There needs to be communication first before you can start to say what offends you," said one Black student. So, in another student's words, caught in this vicious cycle, "things get buried."

Lack of knowledge is also reflected as the students try to assess racially related experiences. Because most students do not understand enough about each other's histories and cultures, they are often unable to know the potential effects on each other of particular thinking and behavior, especially what has the capacity to hurt on grounds of race or culture. As one White student said, "It's difficult for people of different cultures to understand [each other]. People interpret things differently because of who they are and what they come from." In assessing the original incident, many students of color and White students saw what they described as a "human" incident: "This was an exaggerated response to an act that was not racist. It was a product of misperception." But other students were offended by racial overtones in the situation. And for several Black students, it was an attack on their heritage. Many of the students who saw the incident as a "human situation" were initially unable to understand why others saw the incident as racial in nature. In fact, all these students were correct. It was indeed a "human" incident involving insensitivity of students toward each other. But it also involved racial histories and stereotypes. And that immediately made it a more complicated event.

Specifically, depending on students' relationships to and understanding of African-American history, they viewed the incident in varying terms. In this case, many who initially viewed the situation as a "human" issue began to understand other dimensions as a result of discussions. As several White students observed, "At first I was confused. I didn't see it as a racial issue. Now I do." "I thought the incident was silly. Then I saw Black students in tears and became more involved." "The intentions weren't necessarily racist, but [they were] the result of a lack of cultural understanding." Ultimately, as one student understood, "It's a question of how people *see* it. Not how it *should* be seen." In this case, how it *was* seen resulted in ripple effects that affected the entire community.

Thus in attempting to build the multicultural community in the school, the students are hampered, ironically, by a lack of knowledge—of each other, of language, of concepts, of how to communicate with each other, and of how to assess experience.

The Role of Racial or Cultural Groups

Complicating these larger community dynamics are issues surrounding racial or cultural groups. To some degree, segregated living patterns outside the school give way to segregated groupings within the school. But in the school, what has in many instances emerged quite naturally becomes the object of scrutiny, judgment, discomfort, and confusion. Racially or culturally identifiable groups become a powerful factor in the community, one which is viewed very differently from within the group and from without.

Viewed from within, the groups often represent a community within a community, an inclusive, natural, and supportive social network for the students. As one Black student explained, "It's natural to hang with someone from your background." And as other Black students said, "I appreciate people of the same background for personal sympathy with my problems." . . . "It's hard coming here from an environment where all [my] friends are Afro-Americans of a different economic situation. So it's natural to look to others [who are similar]. That forms groups." . . . One Jewish student said, "Being Jewish, I can understand groups being together. I don't want to say 'assimilate' because I don't want to say you have to lose your culture."

In some cases, a student may be the only one student from a particular race or culture in a particular course. This makes coming back to a group appealing, too. "If you're the only one—White or Black—student in a class, it feels weird," said one student.

In other instances the groups are again a reflection of the gaps among students caused by a lack of knowledge of each other. Said one Black student to several White students, "You don't know me, so I hang with people who can and do."

Groups can also emerge when some students feel excluded by others. As one Latino student explained, "I've gone where I felt welcomed." Or as one Black student said, "The first students who welcomed me here were Black students."

Supportive as they are from within, because the groups form along racial or cultural lines, they are complex viewed from without. The same inclusivity viewed from within the group triggers a sense of exclusivity and discomfort viewed from the outside. As one White student said, "Why are all the Black students hanging around with each other? The answer is another question: Why is it that all the White students sit together?"

For some in the community, the racial or cultural groups have another troubling aspect. Because the groups suggest segregation, they are a symbol or a reminder of something we as a nation have deemed so unacceptable we have been willing to legislate against it to try to eliminate it. As one White student asked, "Why are the Blacks segregated?" In the lingering shadow of the Jim Crow laws, many adults and students in the school are unwilling to allow what appears to be segregation to emerge, even though it can and does serve a positive and supportive function within the community. Many feel it is something which should be discouraged as a vestige of a more racist past. "The school is segregated," said one White student. "People are saying, 'my people and your people.'" And so the groups are viewed uneasily. Because they somehow suggest in an uncomfortable way that we are not the unified community that would be our ideal, the groups get talked about, even as they form naturally, over lunch or leisure or studies.

This uneasiness is intensified if the group identifies itself with a particular political position. To those outside the group, this can be, in the words of one White student responding to the use of Black power chants by a group of Black students, "intimidating" and threatening.

What appears to be the most troubling aspect of the groups viewed from without is that at times they have the effect of dividing the community. To the degree that they nourish those within, they feel as if they exclude those outside of the group. And they leave students feeling that there is ostracism of one group by another. As one White student explained, "We have groups and cliques that alienate each other. Many are formed by race."

Groups and the Individual

Some of the most interesting phenomena associated with group dynamics are those emanating from the relationship of the individual to the group, especially concerning issues of identity and personal responsibility.

The students' observations suggest that group membership confers an identity which can work for or against the individual. The sense of association and belonging that group inclusion provides for those within the group also raises questions for those both inside and outside the group, especially surrounding the questions "Who am I" and "Who is he?" According to these students, personal identity may be assumed, proscribed, or attributed in relation to the group.

Students within a cultural group may struggle, as individuals and with each other, with the degree to which they or their friends assume a public identity and attitude and behavior consonant with the identity of the cultural group. Insecurities about putting this identity into place can divide not only students from different cultural groups but those within the same group. Students may criticize each other for thinking or behaving in a way that reflects a different relationship to the cultural identity. Thus as one distraught young Black student said to another while the original incident unfolded, "How can you say that? How can you care so little for your heritage?"

Students outside the group are also unsure how much group identity and affiliation should control an individual. Said one White student, "We recognize the comfort that groups can provide their members, but we're frustrated with groups trying to impose a code of behavior at the expense of individual rights and privileges and expression. Members inside and outside should maintain an individual freedom apart from the group."

Students are also puzzled over the notion of multiple identities—identities that emerge from self-affiliation with a specific cultural group, and, for the same individual, identities that are national and universal. As one White student asked, "Can you be one thing and another—be African American and part of something larger?" Another said, "[We need to] respect and look at others as people, not as members of a minority group." . . . "Minority students are not just members of a minority group. They are also part of a larger American society."

Students wrestle with how to interact with each other as a result of a sensitivity to the multiple identities of those around them: here Black and White students try to understand how to regard one another. White students: "Should I be colorblind or embrace his ethnicity—or both?" . . . "You *can't* notice or make judgments based on color." A Black student: "You can't be colorblind. You *must* recognize race and learn about other cultures so you can be sensitive to things that will offend." A White student: "When you encounter someone you see race first, then you learn layers of the person and go deeper." As one White student says, trying to figure it out, "First we're a human being, then an American, then a race or religion." But real circumstances around the students continue to make issues of identity confusing.

Additionally, at times, students are expected to generalize about members of a racial or cultural group to be sensitive to issues of racial or cultural identity or heritage. But those same students are expected not to generalize about members of a particular race or culture when it means not being cognizant of the individuality of the student within the group. For example, White students may be expected by Latino students to know that many Latinos may be sensitive to issues relating to immigration. But those same White students may be expected by Latino students not to make presumptions about any given Latino student since those presumptions are not grounded in a knowledge of the uniqueness of the individual and thus may well be erroneous. For some students the challenge becomes that of regarding sufficiently both the individual and the group identity. "We shouldn't talk about 'the Black people,'" said one White student, "[Blacks are] individuals."

Challenges also arise surrounding the individual's responsibility to the group and the cultural identity the group represents. In many instances, from both within and outside the group, students become—whether they like it or not—representatives of their cultural groups. This raises questions inside and outside the group.

Those outside the group may rightly or wrongly confer a racial or cultural identity on an individual, especially because of the ambivalence already surrounding the issue of colorblindness, and see that student as representative of his or her cultural group. As a result, the individual's attitudes and behavior become the basis for making judgments or drawing conclusions about the cultural group as a whole. Judgments about the individual are linked to the larger cultural group. Both White and Black students in the original incident became, in the eyes of some students, representatives of their communities.

This has a whole series of repercussions for the individual. Not only can one individual not represent a group, it places a substantial burden on the individual at a time when he is already challenged by the normal identity issues of adolescence. Students wrestle with this burden and come to interesting conclusions. One series of observations by students suggests the issues involved for them:

First student, a White male: I don't think you have a responsibility to make your race look good. [The students in the original incident] feel terrible that they have to be examples of a whole community.

Second student, a Latino male: It's hard not to feel responsibility for your culture. Cops try to arrest me for absolutely no reason because I'm Hispanic. So I personally want to help my race look better, to succeed.

Third student, a Black male: You really only have responsibility to yourself and laws. But when you think about it, some are denied things because of color. A Black guy riots—someone stereotypes. Therefore any little thing you do or say can change the way people think about [your culture]. Therefore you do have a responsibility.

Fourth student, a White male: Like it or not, one Black here represents all Blacks, mostly because there are fewer [Blacks in the community].

The basis for this conclusion, however, again rests in the students' not knowing enough about each other.

So the students may struggle not only with developing and maintaining multiple identities, but with what those identities mean, for themselves, for their peers inside and outside their group, and for their entire culture. That's a demanding position for students to sustain.

One of the most intriguing sets of dynamics concerns the students who actively reach out across cultural lines to other groups. As one White student suggested, this can foster community: "A conscious effort by an individual or the group to accept another student can start to break down the tension between groups." But in reality, individuals who try to cross the terrain between the distinct cultural groups may meet with hostility which suggests an invisible line between culture groups, one not easily crossed. Black students whose actions or attitudes suggest this movement may be seen, in the words of one Black student, as "sellouts." Similarly, said one White student, there may be "verbal ostracism of Whites who are acting Black." Or as another White student said, "I believe in social diversity. I associate with people from different backgrounds and appreciate the different views that people with different backgrounds can give. I am hurt by a Black person saying that I can't understand." Thus, ironically, those who seek to meld the groups, those who may be the most interested in blurring the distinctions between the groups, may be verbally consigned to a netherworld which belongs to no group at all. This discourages more active blending of the groups and reinforces the existence of separate groups.

Therefore separate racial or cultural groups provide a sense of support and belonging for many students. But their role is often misunderstood by the community. And without a clear understanding of that role, the groups may divide the community. They may also at times inhibit expression and free movement of individuals within the larger community. So the groups at times coexist in uneasiness. As one White student remarked, "There is social separation in school and outside." Or as another said, "Everyone puts up walls and is afraid of roaming to find new friends."

The Need for Role Models

In the face of these challenges, many students are actively seeking guidance from adults. But they are also skeptical about the role models they have around them for coping with racial and cultural issues. This means that they are uncertain about whom to rely on.

Models for approaching social issues are provided initially for children in the home. But generally segregated living patterns mean that there may not be models at home for interacting across cultural lines. Or, for some students, the models provided there are not fully workable in the community that is today's school. For example, in an ironic twist of history, White children raised in accordance with the vision of Martin Luther King, Jr.—to be colorblind—are faced with the need in school to recognize color. Said one White student, "You can't ignore people's color. There is a difference between being aware of color and being racist. Some people don't want you to be blind to their culture." So some students, raised according to what worked well for their parents, may be baffled by the reality of contemporary social needs.

Within the school, choices made by adults may trouble and confuse the students. Actions taken by faculty or administrators to help particular students are sometimes construed by other students as separatist and divisive. Said one White student, "Black authority figures are at times just working with Black students and separating the races." Another said, "When teachers segregate students, they add to the problem." Students also recognize that adults around them may not provide the best or most useful examples of cross-racial or cross-cultural interaction. "It's difficult to know who's right," said one student. "We can't blindly follow authority figures."

Thus students may feel perplexed by those around them whom they depend on to provide guidance in a crucial area of their lives. As a result, they are needing, to some degree, to chart the area themselves, by trial and error, without the fully workable examples of adults.

The Short-Term Effects of the Incident

In the wake of this incident and the discussions it evoked, what were the short-term effects for the students?

For many, the experience, while not a comfortable one, was ultimately a productive one. Initially, many of the students were angry or hurt—by what appeared to them to be racism or accusations of racism. And they were afraid of what they witnessed around them and what they felt. "I felt fear for the student body," said one White student. . . . "I fear not changing myself. In what way can I take personal responsibility for what's happening?" asked another.

Students also expressed surprise, even shock, at what the incident and the discussions taught them. Said one White student, "I was surprised. These issues needed to come out. I didn't understand [the issues] at the time. I understand more now."

But as painful as it was at times, many students felt the incident and its aftermath served several constructive functions in the community.

Some students felt that pressure had built up among the students and the incident provided a necessary release of tensions, a community catharsis. As both students of color and White students suggested, "Problems were brewing. There was tension. Good discussions followed. It was good that this came out."

The incident also raised the awareness of many students about each other's situations and feelings, especially in providing White students a greater understanding about the perspectives of students of color. Said one White student, echoing an observation expressed by many, "It's good that this happened. I learned from the discussion. I didn't know how the Black students felt." Or, as another student said, "The Black students opened my eyes. I thought there were no problems. I was totally oblivious." For others, it provided a better understanding of the nature of racism.

Many students suggested the incident raised important questions for them and gave them an opportunity for reflection, for greater understanding of self and others, and for growth. "Discussions were terrific," said one, "so meetings of different races are important." Perhaps this comment, made by a White female, expressed it most fully: "I wanted to ignore the incident at first. But this scared me. I stopped myself and opened my eyes to events and even to terminology that is racist. I saw my own [behavior] as at least discriminatory, if not racist. I've tried to back away from my fears to [try to] overcome barriers."

Although the observations of these students were prompted by one incident in an urban high school, those of us who work with students know this is far from an isolated occurrence. What can such a moment, and the reflections that followed, teach us? In the wake of such moments, we need to listen to the students, to think about what they have placed before us, and to act.

AN INITIATION INTO
CONTEMPORARY AMERICAN LIFE

Incidents like the one that occurred in this high school and the discussions following it serve as an initiation for students into a significant aspect of contemporary American life. The cultural dynamics and challenges revealed by these students' actions and observations are the same as those vexing our national communities.

In discussing his play *Death and the Maiden*, Chilean-American playwright

Ariel Dorfman suggests that the history of a country not only lives in the present, but forces upon people a series of formidable questions: "What do you do with the past in order to construct the future? If you remember too much you may be captured by it. But if you don't remember enough, you may be erasing your origins" (S. Smith, 1993, p. 5). "How can those who tortured and those who were tortured coexist in the same land? How do we forget [the past] without risking its repetition in the future? What are the consequences of suppressing that past and the truth if it is whispering or howling to us? How [do we] confront these issues without destroying the national consensus which creates democratic stability?" (Dorfman, 1993, p. 9). Although Dorfman is writing from the backdrop of a Chilean military dictatorship, the questions he poses about the effects of history reflect the same uncertainties posed by our students.

As Studs Terkel discovered in his recent series of interviews on race, the need to know one's history is deeply haunting, and a knowledge of the past is an essential tool for better living in the present. As one Black man he interviewed suggested, "Unless you go back to the roots and begin to tell the truth about the past, we'll get nowhere. . . . I don't know where the story will end, but we are all kind of messed up" (1992, p. 10). Terkel himself suggests that a full rendering of history is essential in addressing issues of race and culture. In speaking of Emmet Till, the young Black who was murdered in Mississippi, Terkel says, "Those of a certain age, both black and white, remember the boy's name and the circumstances. Neither this knowledge nor its significance has been passed on to today's young. . . . It is not a commentary on them so much as on our sense of history. Or lack of it. . . . In order for us, black and white, to disenthrall ourselves from the harshest slavemaster, racism, we must disinter our buried history" (1992, p. 18). And as psychologists have always understood, connections to the past can enable us to better understand ourselves and others.

Students are also mirroring the lack of understanding across cultures that permeates the national community. As Douglas Massey says in a remark bearing uncanny resemblance to an observation made by one of the high school students, "I don't think most whites understand what it is to be black in the United States today. They don't even have a clue" (Terkel, 1992, p. 95).

The students' concerns with language and communication also echo unresolved issues in the larger culture, ones that have far-reaching practical implications for us all. Slaves felt they had to use coded language to survive the system. But centuries later, according to a recent article in *The New York Times*, race is still so difficult to discuss publicly that politicians run from it. "Race remains a four-letter word in politics, which has prevented all but a few public figures from openly dealing with issues considered too sensitive to discuss because of their real or imagined racial implications" (Roberts, 1993, p. 3). Tensions surrounding town meetings as part of President Clinton's national initiative on race underscore the fact that communication about these issues is far from easy for adults. And as journalist Itabari Njeri explains, "There are few safe places where oppressed groups can express their distress. . . . Instead, much of that rage is turned inward . . . or directed toward those equally or more marginalized . . . " (1993, p. 32).

One of the most moving accounts indicating the presence of these concerns in the national community is a reflection by a Yale Law School professor on the supportive role of cultural groups. Looking back from midlife, this professional still remembers the significance and crucial role of the "black table" during his years as a student. His words underscore the nature of the support provided by close affiliation with one's own cultural group:

> . . . the "black table" (as we called our solidaritied corner of the dining hall) . . . itself was a statement of need, and of difference. We were law students, but we were not like everyone else, or at least we didn't think we were. . . . The gray corridors and cavernous classrooms of the Yale Law School were familiar but never home. . . . As black law students, we had other needs, as well, needs that seemed to us, at least, not exactly the same as the needs of other students. The need to escape, for example. The need to seek support from each other. The need to be together. And the need to figure out exactly what we were doing there, what our *purpose* was, led us into the fierce but friendly debate over just who we were. . . . We were in it together, united by the awarenesses that our shared skin color made possible and the eagerness to know what was right, and no matter how vehement our political differences, the black table remained an axis around which our small worlds revolved. The ease of it all—I miss the ease. . . . Our community seems more divided now, but that perception might represent the fresh perspective that comes when, at last, one must leave the table behind. The *need*, however, is as deep and nagging as ever. (Carter, 1993, pp. 55–56)

In a darker vein, journalist Njeri warns what can happen in our communities when those from different cultural groups are unable to reach across the distances that separate them, to work together. The observations come from an aide in the office of the mayor of Los Angeles before the riots which were to underscore the need to lay the foundations for meaningful connections between cultural groups. "Even when people of apparent goodwill try to cooperate . . . there is this 'impenetrable veil' of hostility, based on ethnic stereotyping, that undermines joint economic and cultural ventures. Traditional mediation and bridge-building efforts," Njeri writes, "are too superficial to penetrate that veil. They don't get at the psychological terror, fed by bigotry [that leads to violence]" (1993, p. 31).

The challenges of multiple identities, too, noted by the students, exist well beyond the school. In *The Souls of Black Folk*, W. E. B. DuBois wrote, "[The Negro] ever feels his twoness—an American, a Negro; two souls, two thoughts, two unreconciled strivings; two warring ideals in one dark body, whose dogged strength alone keeps it from being torn asunder. The history of the American

Negro is the history of this strife—this longing . . . to merge his double self
. . . " (Early, 1993, p. xviii). Gerald Early, Director of the Department of Afri-
can-American Studies at Washington University in St. Louis, feels that the di-
lemma articulated by DuBois in 1903 remains so germane an issue for African
Americans, he asked 20 scholars to respond to the passage in personal essays.
The result, *Lure and Loathing*, is a contemporary meditation on "race, identity,
and the ambivalence" surrounding assimilation in the contemporary African
American community (1993).

Prominent figures have also spoken out recently on the ways in which people of color must grapple with the weight of being cast as representatives of
their culture. "It is not uncommon," explains Wilson J. Moses, Professor of
English and History at Pennsylvania State University, "for us to feel that we are
ambassadors for the race, and that we must achieve by our examples the mighty
task of racial vindication. We feel that if we reveal small human flaws we will
provide excuses for discrimination against all black people. We fear that any
mistakes we make, any deficiencies we reveal, will reflect poorly on our black
colleagues, or make the path worse for black students. We have an irrational
dread that, if we are mediocrities in our profession, we will hold back the progress of the entire race" (Moses, 1993, p. 289). Certainly this is one reason the
Anita Hill–Clarence Thomas hearings inspired such lengthy commentary and
analysis.

Additionally, there is the awareness in the larger culture, as with our students, that there is difficult and risky terrain to cross for those who seek to meld
the groups. After the riots in Los Angeles, the Black minister of one of the
largest Black churches in the city was allegedly targeted in an assassination plot
by White supremacists for his role in helping rebuild community relations. And
as journalist Njeri suggests in considering ways to help bridge the gaps between
groups, "We should, as well, reconnect with allies in the White community. The
latter are often marginalized by their own community when they take progressive and honorable stands against racism" (1993, p. 34). Among adults as well
as adolescents, those who reach across the spaces that divide us are placed at
risk by those who reject such gestures.

Thus, in the words of playwright Arthur Miller, "Attention, attention must
be finally paid . . . " (1949, p. 56). Helping students address these same challenges as they have emerged in our schools means greater hope for creating
workable national communities in the future.

RESPONDING TO THE CHALLENGES

Moments like the racial incident in this high school offer extraordinary opportunities for educators. As the discussions revealed in the wake of this incident,
students are asking for help. And they are asking for help with a crucial, sophis-

ticated aspect of their lives and ours: the building of a workable democratic community. Dewey has suggested that "problems are the stimulus to thinking," that the problems should grow out of "conditions found in present experience" of the child, and that meaningful education "arouses in the learner an active quest for information and for production of new ideas," (Dewey, 1963, p. 79). Further, in admiring the approach of Maria Montessori, he notes, "the real object of education consists in furnishing active help to the normal expansion of the life of the child" (Dewey & Dewey, 1962, p. 107).

What we witness in the aftermath of this racial incident is the purest form of Dewey's vision of the ripeness of an educational opportunity. Out of the students' present experiences emerged real problems and real questions, as well as new ideas as they began to search for answers. In that process they turned to us. We need to seize such situations as stellar moments for education.

The Students Respond

In the discussions following the incident, the students themselves made many suggestions that have considerable merit. Such ideas deserve careful consideration and a response.

Many students felt compelled to act. As one said, "We need to try to expose [the problems], as difficult as it is. We have to learn about [the problems] and live with each other." And another said, "If you choose to ignore [the problems], that becomes part of the issue."

In some cases, pessimism or idealism dominated their suggestions. Some said with resignation, "There is little to nothing we can do about racism." And others, eager to find common ground, suggested, "we shouldn't talk about differences" at all. They also at times felt, in the glow of youth, that anything is possible: "We need to strive for an ideal community within the school."

Other suggestions have not resulted in success in other settings. One such suggestion was increasing the number of students of color in the school *in order to* reduce grouping and stereotypes. Although increasing the number of students of color in the school is an important goal for hosts of reasons, anecdotal evidence suggests that in schools with higher percentages of students of color, similar dynamics still exist.

But many of their suggestions, as well as their overall grasp of the situation, were realistic. As one student said, "There is no immediate solution. This is a process. Start now."

Many of the students were interested in learning more about history: "We need curriculum that exposes us to multicultural issues and how to deal with them." "[We need to be offered] more courses on race and culture." Some students suggested that a course with such a focus be mandatory.

And many students expressed an interest in understanding ways to live with history: "It's important to remember where we came from, but not segregate ourselves." "[We need a balance] between remembering the past and living for the future. [We need to] take lessons, but not hatred, from the past."

Many of these students wanted to learn to communicate with each other about these issues: "We have to learn better ways of communicating." After all, said several, "We need to interact. We need each other." "We have to learn better ways of talking about things. We must [learn ways of communicating that are kinder]."

Several students suggested taking action on several fronts: Said one, "It comes to communication and knowing each other's backgrounds. If I study some of her history and culture, I can understand a lot. I can't know it, but I can understand more."

These students urged gestures that show an understanding of the need for group affiliation as well as the need to knit together as a community: "Students of minority groups should maintain and be proud of their heritage but not use it as a barrier to isolate themselves," said one student. "[We should all] identify with each other," offered another. And another thought, "Students should make it a priority to find out what is important to each group."

They also urged a recasting of common decency for a new age: "Show sensitivity to cultural and class issues." "Be open minded." "Put yourself in the focal point. Ask yourself: 'How would I feel?'" "Make an effort to get to know each other." "Reach out. Have lunch. Make new friends." "Learn to forgive and forget. We need each other. It takes so much effort to hate someone. We have to learn to work with people."

And they were interested in using multiple aspects of school life to address the challenges: "We could use student government as a forum for discussing social issues." "[We can] use what we learn in this community to help in community service, and use what we learn in community service to help here."

We should not underestimate their thinking. Their observations show wisdom and resilience, imagination and sensitivity. Their thinking gives us reason for hope and for optimism.

A TRANSFORMATIVE MOMENT

And so we return to the original incident that unfolded on that morning in spring. Within a few days, several White members of the Video Club had approached a Black teacher for help in understanding what had erupted so unexpectedly in the auditorium. The young Black women had talked and come to accept (even if they did not fully understand) each other's differing relationships to their identities and heritage. Then they had taken their model of rapprochement before their classmates at an assembly intended to address the events of the week before. In the aftermath of an intense, discomforting, and confusing moment, students and adults had been able to learn more about themselves and each other, as well as their community.

A transformative moment had occurred in the lives of the students and in the life of the school. Now the real work continues: acting on the lessons that emerged in the wake of one spring day as students came together to enjoy a series of prize-winning videos.

CONCLUSION

If properly addressed, incidents like the one that erupted on that spring morning in an urban high school have the capacity to better our communities. As the discussions following the original incident pointed out, significant challenges lie before us in helping students create a school community which more closely approximates our historical vision of ourselves as a society.

The incident and the discussions that followed it reveal a confluence of factors in contemporary American life that are experienced every day by many of our students. We have tended to believe that the kind of knowledge that will help them live their daily lives in harmony with each other across racial or cultural lines will happen naturally and automatically. Or we offer up platitudes as palliatives. To do this, however, is contrary to what we and our students know to be true in our school communities. Not to acknowledge the current social terrain is to engage in denial. And as these students themselves have said, "If you choose to ignore it, that becomes part of the issue."

Understanding the specific cultural dynamics in our schools, however, can enable us to address them in ways that will help our students today and in the future. There is a saying familiar to parents that when our children behave the worst, they need us the most. If, in failing to understand or grapple with issues that also vex our brightest thinkers and our most sophisticated national communities, our students provoke an incident or explode with emotion, they are calling on us, in whose care they reside, to help them. In responding, we must be neither impatient, nor critical, nor punitive, but work with them in building communities that can enliven and sustain us all.

CHAPTER 2

THE OPENING OF THE AMERICAN MIND

Challenges in the Cross-cultural Teaching of Literature

In the plush lobby of a corporate auditorium, Gwendolyn Brooks beams as she autographs books of poetry for a waiting line of children, her gentleness radiant. A few moments later, she stands before a nearly all-White audience reading line after line of verse directed at the corrosive and deadly effects of White racism, all in the dignified and polite confines of a public reading.

While the psychological complexities and ironies attendant to this public and literary occasion may be brushed aside as the reading ends, this is not the case in the daily cross-cultural encounters in today's classrooms. The artistry of works by writers of color, the pluralistic nature of the American experience, and the rich challenges found in exploring these works compel us forward in the teaching of writers of color. But contrary to Allan Bloom's fear that any divergence from the "great books" represents a closing of the American mind (1987), the teaching of works by writers of color to integrated classes by White teachers raises complex issues we as educators have yet adequately to address, and demands an opening of the American mind in ways we are just beginning to understand.

Henry Louis Gates, Jr., remembers the response he was given at Cambridge University in the early 1970s when he asked if he could write a doctoral thesis on "Black literature": " . . . the tutor replied with great disdain, 'Tell me, sir, . . . what *is* Black literature?' " (1990, p. 12). Since that time not only Black writers, but Native American, Latino, and Asian-American writers have been singled out and recognized as among the best in the country, winning the Pulitzer Prize, the American and National Book Awards, and the National Book Critics Circle Award, and support by the Guggenheim and MacArthur Foundations. They have earned and are gaining, if belatedly, their rightful place in the canon of American literature. With more frequency these works should take their position in English courses throughout the country. Along with this shift in reading lists, however, come new literary and pedagogical challenges for teachers, whether in the preparation of these works or in the dynamics of classroom discussions as groups of students struggle to confront and discuss their lives and their differences.

CONTEXT: DEFINING THE CHALLENGES

The understanding I have gained of the challenges in working with these texts has come from over 20 years of experience in varied settings. Not only each setting, but each class, with its unique racial and cultural makeup, shapes what dynamics will emerge. To offer, therefore, a full narrative of any one class limits the focus to what emerged in that particular class. Thus this essay focuses not on a single class or course, but on a wide range of situations that have arisen in my own work with these texts and that teachers may well encounter as they bring these texts before their students. Although the essay is an attempt to outline issues pertinent to a particular combination of pedagogical, artistic, and cultural factors, it is intended as well to stimulate dialogue through which we as teachers may better serve our students. Many of the questions the essay raises remain unanswered in my own mind.

PREPARING TO TEACH THE WORKS

The first challenges facing us are found in approaching these texts. Preparation for teaching the works of these writers should be extensive. The very nature of works by writers of color demands an understanding not only of the specific works and writers themselves, but as well the unique historical contexts and literary histories from which they emerge. As Houston Baker suggests, the men and women who viewed the New World from the deck of the *Mayflower* saw a different world ahead of them than did those seeing the same world from the holds of slave ships, and these origins led to completely different lives, experiences, perceptions, and relationships to language (1980, p. 156).

From the multiple contrary American experiences grow not only discrete histories and literatures, but myths, archetypes, meanings, significance, and symbols as well. Not to know these is to risk serious misreadings of the texts. Consider the following situations: As C. W. E. Bigsby points out, while twentieth-century White writers found cities oppressive and alienating, Blacks migrating to New York from the rural south found Harlem to be equated with opportunity and community (1980, pp. 16–17). When the reviewer for *Commonweal* reviewed N. Scott Momaday's novel *House Made of Dawn* (1968), he criticized the title for its awkwardness (Standiford, 1982, p. 187). A knowledge of Native-American culture, however, would have allowed him to understand the title as part of a prayer song from an ancient Navajo healing ceremony. Thus, strictly Eurocentric foundations simply do not serve the instructor adequately to approach these works.

CLASSROOM DYNAMICS

Preparing the works is only the initial challenge. Working with these texts with students issues a new set of challenges. Because of the nature of these works, during discussions, students identify with elements of the works in multiple ways. Many of these identifications are significant for their benefits, but along with the beneficial identifications come more complex ones.

In his essay on modern literature, Lionel Trilling argued that "no literature has ever been so shockingly personal as that of our time" (1965, p. 8). In its insistence on political and social realities, modern literature by writers of color provides students of color with opportunities for identification with literary characters and situations denied them throughout the history of American schooling. In a famous 1930s photograph by Margaret Bourke-White, the children of an all-Black elementary school hold in their hands their reader, *The Pathway to Reading*. An excerpt from the reader serves as caption for the photograph: "And so the fairy godmother in the storybook touched the little white girls with her wand and they were all turned into little princesses" (Caldwell & Bourke-White, 1937, unnumbered page). For decades, material used to teach reading and literature to students of color depicted a White world. And as James Banks has noted, "Students learn best and are more highly motivated when the school curriculum reflects their cultures, experiences, and perspectives" (1993a, p. 195). Whatever arguments can be made for the relationship between academic success and self-esteem, students of color have long been denied the opportunity to find themselves and their lives in the works offered by their English departments.

As more and more works by writers of color enter English departments, however, the connections between students of color and literature are palpable. As one Black student remarked recently during a discussion of Gloria Naylor's *The Women of Brewster Place* (1982), "I like Mattie. She reminds me of my mother, who left the rural South and came North into hard times." And as one young Chicana observed during a discussion related to the study of Rolando Hinojosa's *This Migrant Earth* (1987), "You identify more with history when it's your own. My grandfather traveled with great-grandparents moving from Mexico to Texas and working with migrants." One student responded tellingly to a moment in Sandra Cisneros's *The House on Mango Street* (1989):

> The teachers have difficulty pronouncing her name or didn't want to try. I can definitely relate to that. One time a woman asked me my name and I told her. She responded, "Well, I can't pronounce that so I'm just going to call you 'girl.'" To me, it was not her inability to say my name, it was her lack of effort to say my name, like it was unimportant, like I was. My name means "beautiful flower, richly endowed." I'm proud of that. I've tried to live up to that name. It really hurt when she didn't note that the name was

unique, ask me its meaning, or even try to say it. If you can't take the time
to get to know my name, how can you get to know me?

Repeatedly in the process of drafting college application essays, students of
color recall personal turning points and moments of enlightenment triggered by
reading specific writers of color: Sojourner Truth, Zora Neale Hurston, Ralph
Ellison, Toni Morrison, Amy Tan. As Toni Cade Bambara has said of her stories, "I work to produce stories that save our lives" (1984, p. 47). Just as writers
of color have given order to the chaos of life through their stories, many students
find them sustaining.

Whatever the joys of young students finding themselves in these works,
however, the very process of identification has its more difficult side and its
own set of psychological and pedagogical challenges, especially in integrated
classes of relatively few students of color. For students of color these challenges
can be painful. As students of color may be identifying with characters or situations, they may become the representatives, in the classroom, of the population
group under discussion. This may generate awkwardness, embarrassment, or
anger. As representatives of the group in question, they may be linked by their
classmates, however unfairly or unrealistically, with negative characters or characteristics depicted by the writers and may be called upon to answer for or
explain in some way the fictionalized situation. Thus although students of color
may be gaining a literary history, at times they are doing so in front of students
who can be insensitive to a host of issues directly or indirectly associated with
culture and identity. For example, what are the short- and long-term impacts of
one student spontaneously decrying mixed race identity in the presence of classmates from mixed marriages? Knowing little of histories of people of color
leads White students to ask naive or ignorant questions and to make incorrect
assumptions. Intentional or not, these are painful to students of color in the class
and can create awkward or painful moments for individuals or for the group as
a whole. As several students of color faced with life at a predominantly White
preparatory school explained in *Best Intentions: The Education and Killing of
Edmund Perry*: "I remember a white boy in one of my classes. He said, 'Blacks
don't have to be on welfare. Instead of spending all their welfare checks, all
they have to do is invest a little each week'" (Anson, 1987, p. 91). "It was . . .
white ignorance and insensitivity that was so maddening. 'They just don't know
anything' . . . . " (Anson, 1987, p. 153).

White students, too, face difficult moments. Generally, the security offered
by membership in the dominant culture cushions the identification of White
students with what might be considered unflattering situations involving Whites
depicted in the literature. However, as representatives within the class of their
race's attitudes and behaviors, past and present, rightly or wrongly, they may
represent the target of the writer and become the guilty party in racial wrongdo-

ings. This can often lead to palpable discomfort, to defensiveness, and then to remarks, accurate or not, growing out of that defensiveness. The discussion becomes the repository for the collective tensions in the group. Remarks made out of this tension may also provide a backlash against the writer's intention. Said one White student recently of a short story by Hugo Martinez-Serros (1988) about urban Chicano poverty: "I wanted to laugh." The statement immediately alienated those students in the class who have lived their own lives close to poverty and created a palpable division among the students along socioeconomic lines, making it very difficult for the discussion to continue. In such moments, the discussion can become painful exchanges, whether on specific historical acts, persons, or issues. In the wake of these moments, how do students feel? Have they grown? What are the effects?

For some, especially if they are the only students of a particular culture in the class, the focus of the discussion on their own culture may create a discomfort they are unable to articulate. At such times, they may feel the need to absent themselves from the discussion and even from the room. In one discussion of a collection of Chicano short stories (Martinez-Serros, 1988), the sole Latino student in the class, although often a leader in discussions, asked to be excused. He remained absent for the duration of the discussion. The stories had explored the dangers of the pressures of assimilation on Chicano families straddling two cultures.

These works deal with powerful issues which will affect students differently, depending on where students are in their relationship to their own identity and culture. In one discussion of issues involving Blacks, one young Black woman who had attended both predominantly White and predominantly Black schools began to shake uncontrollably as she described what it was like to have few Black friends in the predominantly White school. Spontaneously, an Asian-American student sitting next to her reached out and steadied her arm as she spoke. In another moment, a young Black woman remarked, during a study of Leslie Marmon Silko's novel *Ceremony* (1977), "[When we began this] I thought, 'Not another one of those Indian-and-his-land things.' Then I realized what I was saying: that people must say of me, when I get ready to speak, 'Not another one of those Black struggles things.'"

In many such poignant moments, students are coming to realizations about themselves and others as they speak. They are engaged in open questioning, a tentative searching—of themselves, their classmates, and their society—for answers. Some are visibly taking their first steps in clarifying for themselves personal issues of identity and culture, and are doing so in public. In such moments as these, we teachers and our students are *watching* education take place, viscerally, in a classroom.

Several additional factors coalesce to make discussion of these issues complex and difficult.

Thomas Kochman, the author of *Black and White Styles in Conflict* (1981), has noted that as a culture we lack "the public etiquette to talk about differences" (private workshop, Fall, 1990). Perhaps aware of this on some level, many adults in this culture often simply avoid engaging in such cross-cultural discussions because they can be awkward, tense, or unsatisfactory. Young people, then, lack the appropriate models for this process—both individual role models and a model of the process. Nowhere is this more painfully and movingly clear than in classrooms of children whose honesty still dominates their impulses and whose social skills lack the restraining influences found in adults.

In an article examining aspects of Chicano identity, Carlos Arce makes the point that "self-labeling" of population groups is constantly in flux and evolves with evolving social changes. Thus at one point Chicanos might identify themselves as "Chicanos" and at another as "Mexican-Americans" (1981, p. 183). Similarly, over the years, Blacks have been "Negroes," "Blacks," "Afro-Americans," and "African Americans."

The combination of these factors means that students lack a model in the culture for engaging in a discussion of these issues, the role models to show how it's done, and the language, the nomenclature, even, with which to conduct the discussion.

Consider the struggle for models and language that appears in the following fragment taken from an actual discussion:

A White student addressing Black students: I'm confused. I'm afraid to offend you. What should I call you? I was raised to be colorblind. What do Blacks want?

A Black administrator the students had asked to meet with them in class: If you are colorblind, you erase the special needs a race might have. It is easier to be cultureblind than colorblind. Most kids here *are* colorblind, but African Americans aren't colorblind and can't be. We can't ever forget we're different from you. We are constantly reminded of who we are. There is never a time we can forget who we are or what color we are.

White Student: It's such a hard thing. Everyone wants to do the right thing. What words should I use? Black? Negro? It's hard not to hurt people's feelings. It's about being human to other people.

In this conversation, students, with teachers and an administrator, search together for comfortable language with which to speak to each other and take some of their first steps in engaging in honest dialogue with each other, across cultural lines, *about* each other's identities, fears, and uncertainties.

Multicultural classes embody the unresolved tensions of the larger culture, and these often emerge during the discussion of these works. With particularly sensitive issues, instead of the group as a whole focusing on the work, the group may divide along racial or cultural lines and become confrontational, eyeing each other with suspicion, resentment, and distrust, or engaging in eye-rolling or even name-calling. In these instances, in some way the work or the discussion has tended to draw out dormant, unresolved tensions between White students and students of color. And in these instances, the work ironically has served to underscore or even create distance between individuals rather than to facilitate understanding or closeness.

Thus each stage of discussing the issues raised by these writers may be difficult. Initially, it may be hard simply for students to know how to ask questions of each other, or to feel comfortable in initiating dialogues with each other. This uncertainty or reluctance has an inhibiting effect on the discussion, producing a tentativeness in even the most vocal students. Tensions or uncertainty may make students withdraw from the discussion as it unfolds, leaving important questions unasked, important voices and perspectives unheard. In one recent instance, each Black student in a particular class was reluctant to have his very good narrative writing read aloud. Each paper had focused on an issue related to race. Additionally, anticipating the tensions that accompany discussions about these issues may make students avoid even taking a course in which such discussions are likely to occur. If these discussions occur only in courses *elected* by the students, they may miss altogether the opportunity to gain an understanding about each other or to develop the models and the ways of communicating with each other about issues crucial to the well-being of us all.

Students sense (and they are correct) that they are often unable to engage in comfortable dialogue with their classmates about these issues. And are we adults, in fact, asking children to engage in that which we ourselves are often unwilling to do? We must, as educators, however, push ahead in addressing these dilemmas and in helping our students address them. The stakes are too high, the rewards are too great not to. One recent dialogue emerging in a course on issues of race and culture underscores this point:

First student: America is a White country. The business world is White. How do we all—Native American, Afro-Americans, etc.—live on the same block? . . . The minorities are stuck. Is it living one culture at home and putting on a new face and going to work? How can these cultures unite to make one culture? There is one of me at school and one of me at home.

Second student: What can be done?

Third student: How much in the work force is due to racism? To separatism? What's the system? And what should it be?

Fourth student: The whole thing about race and oppression is becoming aware of choices and decisions.

Here, despite the initial awkward, tense moments, these students have been able to move ahead and frame, with each other, some of the central questions currently facing this country. Such are the potential rewards, ultimately, of teaching these works.

PERSPECTIVE, POWER, AND PEDAGOGY

Against the backdrop of these complex classroom dynamics, White teachers of works by writers of color face a very specific set of challenges centering around issues of perspective and power which ultimately raise the question: How successful can we be? Gwendolyn Brooks has written, "There is indeed a new black today.... And he is understood by *no* white. Not the wise white; not the Schooled white; not the Kind white. Your *least* pre-requisite toward an understanding of the new black is an exceptional Doctorate which can be conferred only upon those with the proper properties of bitter birth and intrinsic sorrow" (1972, p. 85). If this is so, how can the White teacher understand the student of color well enough to make wise choices in selecting writers or designing courses given the wealth of material available, or to understand the effect a particular work may have on a student of color? For example, what may be the effect on very dark-skinned children of a discussion led by a White teacher of Gwendolyn Brooks's poem "The Life of Lincoln West," about a very dark-skinned child struggling with his identity? Are there works that, given the dynamics in integrated classrooms, should *not* be taught *because* of the sensitive nature of the racial issues the works raise? Or is it being racist even to pose these questions?

In teaching these works, the White teacher leaves the comfortable position of the insider and the security of known critical assumptions, myths, archetypes, and histories. The White teacher is approaching these works as an outsider, one who has neither felt nor lived the experiences under consideration. While this could also be said of someone approaching works of earlier ages or cultures, the distance that separates contemporary, discrete cultures within the same country may be more difficult to traverse, burdened as it is by proximate issues of politics and power. From this position of the outsider, the teacher must initially justify his relationship to the material, to establish himself as trustworthy. As Cary Wintz points out, even during the Harlem Renaissance, a period of unprecedented intermingling of Blacks and Whites interested in writing, "... White involvement ... always generated a certain amount of suspicion and resentment" (1988, p. 155). "There were always elements that strained the relationship ..." (1988, p. 189).

Although the White teacher's membership in the dominant group confers a type of security in the face of examining the issues raised by writers of color, this position also carries with it the danger of appearing to speak from a position of hypocritical loftiness. What does it mean for the White teacher to lead an analysis of a story about the effects of poverty on children of color among a group of students some of whom know poverty first hand? In this instance, does calling attention to this problem from the relative ease of the culturally dominant position carry with it unavoidably a quality of dispassionate judgment or hypocrisy? Is it possible to navigate successfully the fine line which separates the appropriate tone of teacher as literary critic from the damaging tones of patronizing condescension or clinical coldness? Further, the outsider perspective carries with it the danger of apparent voyeurism and, always, the danger of ignorance. The teacher can only guess what may come across as racist. In discussing Richard Wright's *Native Son* (1940), will it sound racist to raise questions about the Black church as historically an instrument of social control serving White masters, when it is seen by Black students in the class as one of the primary elements of support in the Black community? As a representative of the group being targeted in much of the literature, the teacher may be seen as guilty by association, and this potentially increases his or her discomfort and vulnerability as instructor. Additionally, Houston Baker contends that the questions raised by the White modern writers Trilling found so intimately relevant, even "spiritual" (Trilling, 1965, p. 9), may not be relevant at all to a reader outside the middle class White Western mentality (Baker, 1987, p. 6). Therefore, can we as White classroom critics even pose the right questions of these works?

However, the degree to which the teacher perceives and experiences his or her position as the outsider may also be the degree to which he or she can begin to understand what students of color have long experienced. And an awareness of the separation between cultures and the notion of separate communities of writers also raises our awareness of how exclusionary past assumptions and practices may have been. Such a reference, on the part of the White teacher, as "our friend Sandburg," offered as a gesture of community, may have only underscored the degree to which some members of the class were not members of that community.

Perhaps one of the greatest challenges lies in drawing the distinction between the literary and the personal in the natural process of literary criticism central to discussions of the works. Judging writers, characters, or situations may be quickly perceived by students as rendering judgments on the cultural or racial group with which they are identified, and thus as making an implicit or explicit criticism of behavior or values of that group. Gloria Naylor's treatment of single motherhood in the story of Cora Lee in *The Women of Brewster Place* (1982) is a case in point. Even allowing the criticism of Cora Lee's mothering to come solely from the author herself little mitigates the often stinging criticisms, and then, in response, the defensiveness and lingering discomfort the story elicits during discussions. This points to the difficulties of engaging in that which is by nature judgmental, while finding and using language that is not or does not appear judgmental about the racial or cultural group represented in the works.

Issues of power further complicate the teacher's role. In the classroom, the (White) teacher has de facto power and control over the students (of color). This, at least theoretically, replicates the distribution of power in the larger culture which has been historically negative and destructive from the point of view of people of color. The White teacher is also in a position of being the spokesperson for writers of color. If the teacher is ultimately the arbiter of taste, choice, and judgment, he or she still subordinates even the most radical writers under his or her control. And as C. W. E. Bigsby has pointed out, for Blacks historically, "language was an essential part of the process of manipulation and control." Suppression of another's language was "the essence of" enslavement (1980, p. 40). In the case of the White teacher, the language of literary criticism and discourse is the language of the oppressor. Thus the degree to which students of color are "educated," that is, conscious of history, is the degree to which they may wish to reject the White teacher as a source of instruction. Ironically, then, the greater the success of the teaching, the greater the potential for the student to reject the messenger who has brought the message of oppression. Bigsby has written about White critics of Black literature: "The point was that black art was to be addressed to blacks, and the presence of white intermediaries was too familiar an act of cultural appropriation to be tolerated" (1980, p. 52). As the mediator between the literary work and the students, the White teacher may become the unwanted intermediary in communication among people of color, symbolically or actually insinuating himself or herself into situations where he or she is not wanted.

THE LITERATURE ITSELF

The nature of the works also yields challenges. As Julius Lester said, "If the black artist does not commit his art to the liberation movement . . . he is not fulfilling his responsibility" (quoted in Bigsby, 1980, p. 49). Works by writers of color are often politically charged ones that evoke strong responses. Because of their impact on students, their power makes them more complicated to address than works grounded in a greater psychological or historical distance. Discussions of Nathaniel Hawthorne or Herman Melville, even Kurt Vonnegut, Raymond Carver, or Tillie Olsen, rarely provoke the tensions that ensue in discussions of James Baldwin, Toni Morrison, Amy Tan, Leslie Marmon Silko, or Rolando Hinojosa. In the larger community, these writers are controversial as well. In a recent discussion on National Public Radio, a spokesperson for the Heritage Foundation, a conservative Washington think tank, referred to the growing multicultural education movement (and its reliance on non-Western texts) as racist. Thus although today's writers of color are, in some circles, suspect for their political content, rarely have the tables been reversed: who, in large public arenas, has publicly protested the teaching of Hemingway for his patently racist references to Native Americans in the Nick Adams stories?

For all of us, teachers and students, in and out of classrooms, the works of writers of color make us answer for our choices and behavior in the past and today, and confront uncomfortable truths. These are iconoclastic works. To teach Toni Morrison's novel *Beloved* (1987) is to face, on the part of Whites, our historical role in brutal acts reminiscent of those during the Holocaust. Perhaps no other group of writers makes so clear the discrepancy between what we say we are as a country and what we are. Very often this is a literature of suffering, and we are called upon to answer for that pain.

CONCLUSION

In our multicultural classrooms, White teachers will increasingly work with students of color. As Geneva Gay has noted, "Whites [already] far outnumber minorities in all . . . instructional positions" (1993, p. 173). And as James Banks and Cherry McGee Banks have pointed out, "While the percentage of students of color in the nation's schools is increasing rapidly, the percentage of teachers of color is decreasing sharply" (1993, p. 169). Thus we must have the background and the resolve to offer an accurate rendering of the American experience in and through the teaching of literature by writers of color. And we must begin to understand and address more fully the multiple challenges these works pose in a classroom. The better we understand the challenges, the better we can serve both students and authors. As Houston Baker observed in the preface to a collection of essays on Native-American, Chicano, and Asian-American literature, "Without a sound knowledge of [literature by writers of color], one cannot arrive at a just assessment of the distinctive character of American social and intellectual history" (1982, p. 2). And as Frederick Douglass said over a hundred years ago, "If there is no struggle there is no progress." As teachers, we owe it to our students to continue that struggle toward progress.

CHAPTER 3

READING THE TEXT OF THE TALKING

A Novel Approach to Understanding the Impact of Cultural Divisiveness on Adolescents

In both Toni Morrison's *Beloved* (1987) and William Styron's *Sophie's Choice* (1979), seminal works about slavery and the Holocaust, respectively, profound racial and cultural animosities in the lives of adults produce devastating consequences in the lives of children. In both instances, children are sacrificed in bitter moments of lingering cultural warfare. Although the fates of the children of slavery or of the concentration camps of Nazi Germany are far removed from contemporary America, children's lives today still bear the burden of a world shaped by racial and cultural divisions. American children today are struggling under burdens imposed by their cultural histories and the divisiveness of a world they inherited but did not make. Those burdens are complicating their coming of age and their ability to forge a sense of belonging in the larger community of their peers.

One arena in which this is particularly evident is in the discussions unfolding daily in today's multicultural classrooms. Similar to Morrison's and Styron's dense and compelling novels, the students' discussions provide us with a text—complete with structure and substance—reflecting the complex and troubling impact of cultural divisiveness on the young. It is a text which reflects the idealization of schooling and dialogue as well as the disillusionment with them as instruments of understanding, and it contains the sometimes brilliant but often failed moments of attempts at reparation in the face of the tensions in the larger culture. It is also a text which can be read and analyzed and offered up as a rationale for urgent needs in American schooling.

The analysis that follows focuses on one series of discussions that erupted spontaneously in a class on twentieth-century fiction. Names and identifying details have been changed to protect the privacy of the students.

THE TEXT EMERGES

"If *you* were telling a story about this history, about this event," I asked, "how might you tell it?"

In one segment of a course on contemporary literature, students explored several philosophical and artistic responses to World War II and the Holocaust and considered how they might grapple artistically with the past. After we had viewed *Night and Fog*, Alain Resnais's stark documentary on concentration camps (1955), I had posed a question about their concepts of writing about that era. It was meant to be a morning about stories, and it was. But not what I had imagined.

"I think I would focus on one family—like *Schindler's List*," says one student.

"I don't think I could write about it," says another.

"I've often thought about this," says another, a young woman whose family had come from Eastern Europe. "I think I would reverse it . . . ."

"Why? Tell us more."

Well, she suggests, the Holocaust is given too much attention. There have been other situations. We all know about the Holocaust but not the others. What about the Turks . . . ?

But before she can finish sketching out the structure and rationale of her own fictional approach to history, the emotional tone of the group explodes.

For the next hour, Jewish students, Blacks, an Eastern European, and an Asian weep histories in anger and confusion, clamoring to be known, understood, and soothed, caught between the need to know and be true to their own personal and cultural history and the need to build a community of their peers.

In this particular case, what had begun as an introduction to a contemporary short story ended as a fiercely passionate, antagonistic, and disturbing dialogue about the past and cultural divisiveness. What had been offered as a series of students' fantasies about writing fiction served to release the simmering passions, confusions, and yearnings today's adolescents carry just beneath the surface in a larger culture whose separate cultures exist in an ongoing tension with each other. What ensued was a competition of sorts, of histories of pain, and an indication of what those histories mean in the daily lives of adolescents.

"How can you even let someone make such a statement!"

"There are seventeen people in this room. If someone killed us it would be called a massacre. But six million . . . six million people died, and you say it's 'given too much attention'?"

"I carry so much anger around inside me because of my past, what happened to my people. My grandmother's best friend lost her husband and two children in a concentration camp. If she rolls up her sleeve you can see the tattoo on her arm."

Jewish students are incensed at the notion that the Holocaust could be given too much attention, that such a statement could be permitted.

Black students counter with cries of 100 million in slavery and the ongoing indignities of racism.

And in the midst of it all, a young Asian, trembling, offers her history—a story of bodies and bones, loss and dislocation, immigration, and the reliving of it all through flashbacks. She apologizes, not wanting to offend anyone with her anger.

For a few minutes the room is quiet. Ngim has never before spoken of her life.

Then, in the aftermath of her words, the talking takes another turn. The hostility subsides, and students reach out in an attempt at reparation.

One young Black woman speaks first. "When you say 'my people,' it cuts others off. As though someone cut off his own finger. We're all human beings together. We have to look inside ourselves. When someone hurts me, I pray for them. You could do that when you go to your temple—pray for the ones who hurt you. I say we've got to get together."

But the hostilities have been unleashed, and the wounds are palpable.

With few moments remaining, I try to underscore several suggestions offered for addressing the conflicts, and ask for others. Students suggest seminars, courses. We limp through the final moments. Students leave. The last three deliberately move slowly, perhaps still hoping to bridge the gulfs that cut so deep between them and that they sense so clearly. They linger after the lights are out.

Still disturbed by it all days later, I seek out the advice of colleagues. "If Ngim felt she could say what she said, it's a good class," they tell me. "These things do hurt, because they are real and unresolved." And I recall an observation by James Banks, a leading proponent of multicultural education: "I encourage self-disclosure, but I will not let students hurt each other" (personal communication, 1994).

That's what haunts. That's what's unresolved for me. I fear that in my class students have hurt others and been hurt in the natural flow of discussing the realties of history.

Although such tensions are familiar to anyone working in multicultural classrooms today, the depth of the chasms that often divide our students in the community of the school is troubling. What are we to make of such ragged and unresolved spontaneous discussions?

What I would like to suggest is that such discussions have much in common with the fictional texts that serve as the basis for the course in which this discussion exploded. And they resemble not a simple tale, but the complex text of great literature. If this is the case, what, in fact, is the text of the talking? What does it say? What is its structure? And what are its implications?

The uneasiness among cultures pervasive today and circumscribing the lives of students accompanies them into the classroom and can erupt at a moment's notice. What we witness in the face of that is adolescents being buffeted by opposing psychological and social needs as normal developmental tasks are played out within the context of strong racial or culturally defined identities, groups, tensions, and divisions. Similarly to *Beloved* (1987) or *Sophie's Choice* (1979), what these discussions make clear is that central developmental tasks of the young are stressed by past and contemporary cultural dynamics. Just as do Morrison's and Styron's characters, these students struggle with the burden of the past. And they are attempting to forge adult identities and build workable communities of their peers in the face of cultural divisiveness. A brief look at just a few of the psychosocial elements at play gives us a glimpse of why these discussions are so complex as they emerge in multicultural classrooms today. And, as with fine novels, why they deserve the serious reading of a significant text.

A PAST WHICH CANNOT BE KEPT AT BAY

"I carry this anger around with me all the time because of what happened to my people in the past. I know I have to come to terms with that."
—*Jacob*

One of the most compelling lessons of the text of the talking is the power of the past in these adolescent lives. It haunts and moves them. It frightens and sustains them. Some are compelled to remember it, others to forget it. Fleshed out by the multiple perspectives that come together in multicultural classes, it also has the power to overwhelm and divide them. As one student in this discussion said, "Instead of [placing] blame and [focusing on] the past, we need to work toward the future." But another said: "People *don't* look at history enough. People ignore history and say it never happened. People need to look at it and say we can't do it again. Then we can learn from that." The past influences their interactions. Drawn forward, it occupies a central place in the forum.

In part, the past determines who these students are. Historical events may be attached to or an emblem of their identity: "I am part of that. That is part of who I am. I am, in part, my history."

Also significant is the role history has played in the lives of their families. Was there a looking back in the family that was highly influential, as was the case for several of these young Jewish students? Or more pervasively, a looking forward? Were events of history a prominent factor in the students' upbringing? And what are the students' responsibilities in the face of those events? Have they been charged with remembering and pressing others to do the same? Or have they been pressed to forget? Has there been little to no awareness of the past? Or does the past force its way in, uninvited, as it did for the young Asian, in the form of flashbacks?

Each student nonetheless brings his or her own personal, family, and cultural histories to the group. For many students, the violations and aftereffects of key events in the past have become a seminal factor in the construction of their lives. The events live on through stories and lessons handed down by family and friends, in synagogues, churches, and reunions. Each has a story to tell emerging from the private and public moments of an individual life or plucked from the vast array of experiences that define the history of a family or a specific culture. For some, these stories are emotionally laden and carry with them a pressing need to bare and redress the wrongs of the past. In the discussion in this class, recollecting the horrors of the Holocaust was countered by reminders of the horrors of slavery and the Khmer Rouge. And throughout these sweeping images of history came the more personal stories of the way those pasts have shaped the students' own lives—what has happened to grandmothers, fathers, and themselves.

Memories flood forward in no certain order. They are highly personal, but they are also intrinsically political. And the greater the students' awareness of their implications, the more the stories have the capacity to anger, to frustrate, and to disillusion. They often mirror pasts that were violent and unjust, but it takes no searching for these bright young thinkers to connect those moments with moments or experiences from their own lives, and thus to remind them and us that their lives are still entangled darkly in a mesh of cultural distrust, injustice, and divisiveness.

Further, for many, the recollection and recitation of historical moments prompt an anger which, instead of being assuaged by supportive peers, results in drained frustration. The recollection process is by nature self-absorbed and blind to the needs of others in the group. In reflecting on past and present wrongdoings, the students may yearn for empathy, but because the same process is occurring simultaneously within others tied to their own, different histories, each one is left yearning for the empathy of others, but often unable to provide it or to receive it.

The focus on one's own issues and the simultaneous yearning for an empathy that is for the most part not forthcoming often escalates the discussion into a virtual competition of histories and an inevitable growing discomfort and dissatisfaction. The effect is to leave each student isolated in wrestling with his or his group's history. He is powerless to alter the past and now, apparently, powerless even to enlist the level of understanding and empathy he seeks from his peers. The need to have one's own wound salved is stronger than the ability to acknowledge and address similar wounds of others. The pressing need to come to terms with one's own history gets in the way of expressing empathy for others and thus with fostering group relatedness.

As a result of these factors, discussions can quickly become the repository of searing moments generating passion, anger, resentment, and confusion. The students are living with historical divisions they did not create but which they must learn to navigate and to bridge, even while they are still discovering and attempting to understand their own and each other's cultures and pasts.

In this discussion, the attempt to come to terms with genocidal periods in four separate cultures meant the students initially found little support among their peers across cultural lines to comfort them. Although individual students did make an effort to close the gaps that divided them, by the end of class, this discussion of the past had fractured the group.

CONSTRUCTING IDENTITIES

"I'm African-American. When things happen to me now, I don't know if it's because I'm Black, or what."

—*Tamika*

Beyond the role played by the past and history in the discussion, the text of the talking suggests that cultural divisiveness is complicating the executing of key developmental tasks of the young, especially those surrounding the building of a mature identity. And dialogues may not help.

The following observations, based strictly on personal experiences with classroom dynamics, reflect a growing awareness of a pattern of responses on the part of adolescents as they come together to discuss racial or cultural issues in the context of the cultural divisiveness of the larger society. The ways and degrees to which cultural identity, cultural tensions, and cross-cultural dialogues may shape or impinge upon adolescent development remains an area rich with opportunities for investigation and research. Additionally, while the models of development employed here are familiar ones within a Western perspective (Blos, 1941; Erikson, 1963, 1980; Tatum, 1992), emerging research suggests that to better understand issues of identity and social relations involving students from non-Western cultures—and even from ethnic cultures in the United States—we may need to employ alternative models of development (Hoffman, 1996; Roland, 1988).

One of the essential psycho-social tasks of adolescence is the formation of a stable identity. What discussions like the one that erupted in this class suggest is that a number of the elements Erikson (1963, 1980) has described as part of the process of constructing a mature identity are made more complex by intercultural dynamics today. Letting go of earlier role models, gaining the affirmation of peers, and defending against role confusion all appear complicated by current cross-cultural dynamics. Erikson also noted years ago that the formation of a mature identity is more difficult in a democracy such as ours which demands a "self-made" identity and is characterized by changing conditions (1980, pp. 98–99). If anything, his observation is even more true today, and some of those changing conditions are clearly found among dynamics involving cultural subgroups.

One way in which these dynamics affect adolescent identity formation concerns the questioning of earlier role models as students progress toward the relative independence of mature identity. Instead of facilitating the leaving behind of earlier models, cross-cultural tensions appear to reinforce earlier bonds. Because many students are highly identified with their race or culture, as they engage in discussions across cultural lines, they often experience other students' observations, misunderstandings, ignorant remarks, or criticisms about their culture as attacks on themselves. Defending against that threat has the effect of strengthening the bond to their own culture—and to family and role models within the culture—as they defend against the threat coming from outside the culture. Earlier models provide ballast in the unsettling dynamics of the wider community.

Dynamics in a multicultural community also complicate natural adolescent preoccupation with the opinions of others, and the strong need adolescents have for approval of their peers as they attempt to solidify their emerging identity. In discussions, students are often caught in a double bind. As they speak for and at times defend their own culture, they succeed in strengthening their cultural identity and bonds with peers in their own culture. But affirming their own cultural identity may distance them from peers in other cultures. This leaves students feeling uneasy, since the approval of some peers has been accomplished at the expense of visibly alienating other peers.

Further, the effects of safeguarding against role confusion are rendered considerably more complex amidst the dynamics in a multicultural community. Erikson (1963, 1980) notes that natural and essential defenses against role confusion prompt adolescents to form cliques with those similar to themselves and to engage in stereotyping, intolerance, and exclusion of those who are different. All these gestures can have significant consequences when they are played out in a multicultural setting. The cliques are often formed of individuals from the same or similar cultural groups, and these groups do provide their individual members with identity support and affirmation. However, the formation of these culturally identifiable cliques constitutes a form of self-segregation and cultural separatism in the larger community. Comfort with like peers and discomfort with peers less alike leads to alienation from peers in other culturally defined groups, less interaction with those peers, fewer opportunities to gain understanding across group lines, and less large-group cohesiveness. These larger group patterns foster tensions which deepen the divisions among the cultural groups and solidify the individual cultural cliques in an endless cycle. Here again, to serve one need stresses another, since the cliques strengthen students' individual identities, but the ensuing strengthening of separate culture-groups may also distance or alienate the students from peers or groups of peers in other cultures.

Several of the natural and necessary defenses against role confusion described by Erikson are overtly counterproductive in multicultural settings. Ego uncertainty and the shoring up of fledgling identities, Erikson says (1963, 1980), lead adolescents to stereotyping, intolerance, and exclusion of others who are different, including differences in skin color and culture. This means that students who may unconsciously act out of natural psychological instincts to protect their maturing self may engage in behavior that is distinctly divisive and damaging in a multicultural community defined by hosts of differences among the students. The result of such behavior is, again, the alienation of the very individuals—their peers—from whom they also seek approval. So students may act in ways that are understandable from a private psychosocial, developmental standpoint, to protect their identity, but which directly contradict other, equally pressing, more public psychosocial needs—to win approval of their peers and significant others in their community, and to meet the overall social requirement of the community—that is, to be tolerant.

Additionally, as Erikson (1980) suggested, changing conditions in this American democracy render more difficult the formation of identity. With these students, clearly, among those changing conditions are race relations. Relatively recent research on identity formation suggests that "in a society where racial-group membership is emphasized, the development of a racial identity will occur in some form in everyone" (Tatum, 1992, p. 9). The stages of forming that identity differ, however, for whites and for individuals of color, due largely to the "dominant/subordinate relationship of Whites and people of color in this society . . . " (Tatum, p. 9). The development of racial identity further complicates the already complex tasks described by Erikson.

The formation of a racial identity proceeds through numerous stages, but those stages are not tied to particular psychosocial stages, and movement along the various stages is fluid. An individual may move back and forth through stages. The stage of one's racial identity development influences the way one feels about one's own self and the way one thinks and behaves in relation to those of the same race and to those of other races. Individuals in a group may represent a wide range of stages of racial identity development. As these individuals interact, the difference in their stages may produce conflicts. Some stages in particular can result in difficult dynamics among mixed-race groups. But the students may neither understand nor know how to address the ensuing conflicts. Few students know of the concept of racial identity development or the stages involved, but they do have strong feelings about racial identity—their own and others'. They do not know why they feel as they do or that others experience similar feelings. As Beverly Tatum explains, "The emotional responses that students have to talking and learning about racism are quite predictable and related to their own racial identity development. Unfortunately, students typically do not know this; thus they consider their own guilt, shame, embarrassment, or anger an uncomfortable experience that they alone are having" (1992, p. 19). Tensions in the discussions result from "a collision of developmental processes that can be inherently useful for the racial identity development of the individuals involved," notes Tatum, but the "interaction" may be problematic for teachers and students "unfamiliar with the process" (1992, p. 9).

Last, even dialogues addressing cultural issues can work against the smooth course of adolescent identity development. On one hand, many students believe in dialogues to help them get to know and understand each other across cultural lines, and they want to engage in them. But actually engaging in these dialogues stresses budding identities in several ways.

Many students have been raised to see themselves and their country as just. And many students tend to deny any prejudice within themselves (Tatum, 1992). But in multicultural discussions of race and culture, students hear multiple viewpoints, including potent firsthand accounts of racism. This makes these discussions iconoclastic. Students often discover that their own attitudes and choices are or can be perceived as racist. And they may see their families, their role models, their culture, and their country in a new light, one that is distinctly disturbing. As well, students whose lives have been affected directly by the realities of prejudice and racism are frustrated to hear them denied. Further, individuals are vulnerable to the effects of taking personally observations involving their race or culture. All of these factors can lead to destabilizing moments for adolescents in the process of constructing their identities. Who is right? Whom can I turn to for the truth and for confirmation of my own or my family's or my cultural group's values and behaviors?

Thus, significant aspects of the process of adolescent identity formation described by Erikson appear to be made more difficult by contemporary cultural dynamics. And the result is often, in fact, role confusion.

In this particular discussion, the young woman whose remarks triggered the tensions came from an Eastern European background. The genocide she felt most closely identified with was a massacre by the Turks, an event she felt had gotten little treatment in her education, especially in contrast to the treatment accorded Nazi Germany and the Holocaust.

Because Jewish students in the group were also heavily identified with their culture and its past, however, they reacted strongly to her observation about studying the Holocaust, and the discussion immediately became more intense. In an effort to defend against the threat to their (cultural) identity, they attempted to elicit empathy for the suffering of those in their own culture through observations about the Holocaust. And once stories about the Holocaust poured forth, so did stories about slavery and the Khmer Rouge. These remarks had the effect of re-bonding Jewish and Black students to their own cultures and peers within those cultures, as well as, notably in several cases, their families, but the dynamics also created palpable divisions between Black and Jewish students, between

Black and White students, and between the Jewish peer group and the student whose heritage was Eastern European. The young Eastern European had no group of peers who shared her cultural identity or historical perspective.

In this discussion, cross-cultural dynamics involved adolescents whose nascent identities were embedded in four different cultural traditions. As the conversation grew more complex, these emerging identities were placed in opposition to each other as individual students took differing public stands. Eventually, ensuing tensions had the effects of re-bonding students to earlier role models, disrupting students' relationships with their peers, and, in some cases, clearly creating role confusion. Ironically, this spirited discussion of the past with its tie to cultural identities as well as to cultural divisiveness had stressed rather than supported these students' own youthful and maturing identities.

A COMMUNITY OF ONE'S PEERS

"People are going to get hurt when you talk about issues that are controversial or that they have ties to. You can't avoid anger or hurt."

—*Seth*

Clear also in the text of the talking is that the multicultural milieu of the young affects their ability to construct and maintain a supportive community of their peers.

As Peter Blos noted decades ago, in the normal course of adolescent development, peer groups replace family and school as the most influential factor on their behavior in their movement from childhood to membership in the larger culture. Group opinion and "approval or disapproval of peers becomes progressively the most influential force in motivating adolescent conduct" (1941, p. 249). This involves conflict, says Blos, as it results in the adolescent throwing over certain established modes of conduct, and it requires conformity to the new group of peers. But the peer group also offers security as the adolescent moves from the familiarity of family into the unknowns of adulthood. Even under the best of circumstances the period of adjustment to the wider culture is a difficult time because of its unfamiliar standards and practices, and it will be more difficult in settings where there is heterogeneity of backgrounds (1941, p. 266). The way the adolescent moves through this transition period, says Blos, is significant for achieving maturity.

In multicultural schools, this transitional period may be even more difficult. Coping with the complexities of the larger society may come sooner, since the larger peer group is split not only into smaller peer groups defined by differences in personality or preferences, but into subgroups of various cultures. The larger peer group of these students is a community divided into multiple subgroups defined by unique cultural or racial identities and values. These subgroups may provide a strong sense of ethnic identity and support for individuals within them. But they coexist largely separately and uneasily. Because the subgroup identity is a significant aspect of individual identity, students see themselves as an extension of the subgroup and often experience threats to the subgroup as threats to themselves. This intensifies the nature of interactions between the subgroups (Milton Gordon in Appleton, 1983, pp. 47–48).

Because of the multicultural nature of the larger group, the natural conflict experienced by adolescents in throwing over established models and conforming to a group of peers is accompanied by an additional cluster of inner and outer conflicts. As Nicholas Appleton (1983) explains, in a pluralistic society, inner conflict can be expected to emerge as students opt to be alone; to affiliate with like individuals, which produces minimum conflict; or to choose interactions that produce cultural conflict. Inner conflict also occurs in relation to role identity. How does one meet the needs of both one's own group and other groups? This is especially true for students of color caught between the needs of their subgroup and those of the dominant culture and between their personal wishes and the hopes of their cultural group (Appleton, 1983).

Outer conflict emerges naturally as students interact with peers from cultures unlike their own (Appleton, 1983), with unfamiliar histories, values, and customs. Additionally, relations between groups vary depending on the groups' histories and past and present relations. Vladimir Jankelevitch has suggested that poor relations between groups that are very different are "chilly," but poor relations between groups that are "almost the same" are "highly charged." Among groups where similarities threaten to obliterate uniqueness, identity and self-preservation are secured by stressing differences (quoted in Berman, 1994, p. 62), and this can produce more inflamed interactions. According to Jankelevitch's theory, feelings of ill will between Blacks and Whites may be relatively "chilly," since the two groups have historically regarded each other as "other." But feelings of ill will between American Blacks and American Jews may be charged—the two groups have so much in common historically that they are compelled to assert differences to clarify the uniqueness of their respective identities (Berman, p. 62). These various types of intercultural dynamics are frequently visible among adolescents in classroom discussions focusing on issues of race and culture. But students are rarely in a position to anticipate fully the nature of the interactions that will emerge or to know how to navigate conflictual interactions as they unfold.

In the midst of these conflicts, dialogue plays a paradoxical role. Many students feel strongly about the issues. And many feel a need to talk with each other about them to facilitate cross-cultural cohesiveness. Experience has shown us that dialogues do give students one of the most effective opportunities to know each other better. But for a host of reasons, such discussions may also deepen the divisions among individuals and among the subgroups. Discussions of these issues are typically intense, personal, and volatile. And students have little experience with and few skills for engaging in cross-cultural dialogues about issues so close to their own and each other's lives. Additionally, like the issues they focus on, the discussions elude resolution. As a result, discussions often have the overall effect of dividing rather than uniting the larger group of peers. Like vulnerable identities in these discussions, group cohesiveness takes a beating, even though students idealize dialogue as an instrument for fostering understanding, growth, and closeness.

In the discussion that emerged unexpectedly in the class on contemporary fiction, cultural identity was very strong among students from at least four different cultural groups. As the discussion unfolded, that identity appeared to nudge some students back to their earlier role models and to bind them to their own cultural groups, but it worked against their fostering cohesiveness in the larger community of peers.

Inner conflict and its effects were apparent for a number of students as they articulated positions which put them at odds with peers from other cultural groups, or as they determined which needs to address—personal needs, the needs of their cultural groups, or the needs of the class. This was especially clear with the young Eastern European woman whose perspective on history was shared by no one else, the young Jewish students who reacted strongly to the observations about the Holocaust, the young Asian who had never before spoken openly of her traumatic past, and the young African-American woman who, having taken vocal stands for her own group in discussing the effects of racism and slavery, later shifted focus in an attempt to address the needs of the group as a whole through her words of reconciliation.

Outer conflict became the defining characteristic of the discussion as students from multiple cultures attempted to come to terms with multiple perspectives, and as various types of interactions between the groups emerged. Black and Jewish students divided over what Jankelevitch would say is the effect of being "almost the same" (quoted in Berman, 1994, p. 62). Linked by shared histories of sweeping oppression, they sought to define competitively the differences that distinguished those histories. And in related but different dynamics, African-American students recounting incidents of racist behavior on the part of Whites drew together the African-American students, but strained their relationship with Whites in the class. The origin and nature of the divisive interactions were unique to each pair of groups and emanated from the groups' distinct histories and relations. In practical terms, in a number of instances, these divisions clearly caused students to emphasize bonds with families, previous role models, and peers from their own culture. While this offered the security of the like-peer group, it fragmented the larger group of peers, a group composed of students many of whom were essentially alienated from those racially or culturally unlike themselves.

As I attempted to quell the growing divisiveness and return us to the intended focus for the day, a number of students protested that this discussion was much more important and should continue. Ultimately, however, with students unable to understand the origins and nature of the cross-cultural conflicts unfolding and unable to mediate those conflicts successfully, conflicts divided the group and tensions lingered well beyond the end of class.

Thus the text of the talking makes clear that multicultural dynamics in today's classrooms may work against adolescents' being able to build or maintain a supportive community of peers. The larger group of their peers is beset by conflicts natural in a pluralistic society, conflicts sometimes deepened by the very dialogues students believe in to address them and through which they strive to achieve reconciliation.

TOWARD REPARATION

"I say we've got to get together."

—Jessica

Last, what the text reveals is the strong and pressing need felt by these students to close the significant gaps that divide us all.

Eventually, in this discussion, the intensity of the conversation subsided. Unable or unwilling to tolerate further the tension and confusion that characterized the discussion, the students moved toward conciliation. Students began finding ways to reconnect with each other—they noted hopes they have, strategies for healing wounds, similarities that should bind us; they suggested seminars to hold, courses to offer. As one student said, "We need to quit looking for sympathy and start looking for understanding. I don't want someone to feel sorry for me. I want understanding and knowledge and for [people] to be able to relate to other people." One student tried to address even my uneasiness: "It's not your job to soften the reality. It would make things easier for you to say, 'Let's all agree on this and be happy.' That's impossible. We have to listen and learn."

But ultimately their gestures at reparation were incomplete, unsatisfactory. The chasms they uncovered are larger than they, extend beyond their time, beyond their lives. As for me, the questions this class had raised would haunt me for months.

THE DISCUSSION AS TEXT

What, then, do we make of this spontaneous discussion in a class on fiction? Far from quashing such dialogues, we should recognize and appreciate them as the formidable text they are, a text not unlike that of a fine novel. As with a novel, the discussion these students create has form and content. Dense and intricate, it offers characters, dialogue, and a story—one that shows as well as tells of adolescents in the cultural milieu that is the United States today. It is an elaborate text told not through a single omniscient narrator but through multiple voices, points of view, biases, and perspectives, through monologues and dialogues. It is a fragmented narrative, nonchronological and nonlinear, which moves crablike, following the jagged movement of memory itself.

As with the structure of a novel, the text of the students' discussion arcs from the opening moments through the climax of an emotionally tense and intense weeping of stories underscoring the chasms that frustrate and divide these students. As the weeping subsides, the text slides toward its denouement—a perceived and articulated need for reparation, and a ragged conclusion, lacking closure. The ending is unresolved, unsatisfying, leaving us to ponder the mysteries the text has brought before us, to assemble the disparate chunks, rearrange them, and work out the meaning of parts and the whole for ourselves. Like many great works, it raises more questions than it answers.

As with a text, it can teach, inform, confuse, haunt. Because this discussion-as-text involves describing the past, memories, and human experience, clarity is difficult to achieve; the chance for misunderstanding is high. Like a classic, it is hard, it makes us work.

As with great literature, it can provide therapeutic value for author and reader. As stories of lives, it involves and moves us; it allows us catharsis. It generates both private and public reflection. As with great literature, it is also both a form of and a trigger for public discourse.

As with good works, it lingers in the mind after it's over. The impressions remain: the spent emotion, the felt need for moments of connection, the attempts at reparation, the bridges never achieved, the wounds, the sense of incompleteness grounded in the reality that none of the actual issues are resolved. And as with literature, it has its critics.

Ultimately, however, because it is life and not art, it may leave us with a sense of disorder rather than order, an unresolvable ending rather than the polished leave-taking of a novel.

Just as great writers do, in these discussions our students fashion an exploration of the human condition, both an interpretation of life and a guide to life for us as readers. As with a novel, we can read it, discuss it, interpret it. The more we know, the better readers we will be. As it reflects multiple voices, it admits multiple interpretations. It affects different people differently. It's controversial, and thus it divides us. It is a text full of anger directed at peers who bring the messages that excite, at adults who allow multiple truths to emerge, and at a structure which ultimately provides neither clarity nor answers. But it is also a text full of hope.

Now consider for a moment just a few of the overarching parallels between the text of these students' discussion and an actual text, the text of Morrison's *Beloved* (1987) or Styron's *Sophie's Choice* (1979). In each instance, the larger culture is torn apart by racial or cultural divisiveness, young men and women are haunted by their past and alternately beat it back and allow it to flood their consciousness, and children are victimized by the cultural division in place when they were born. In the midst of attempting to build a life in a world torn apart by such division, the young seek to come to terms with personal, family, and racial and cultural histories, to discover their own identities, and to build a new community. Out of profound disillusionment, they ultimately strive toward reconciliation and a belief in connectedness and the future. Structurally, both the text of the students' talking and the text of the novels are nonchronological observations through multiple perspectives which follow the vagaries of memory. In each case, the reader is left to assemble the pieces. In each case, the work enlightens, moves, and haunts the reader. The echoes of each linger long after the stories are told.

IMPLICATIONS FOR TEACHERS

As we back away from this discussion-as-text, what are its implications—for teachers, and for the larger culture?

The text of these students talking must not be underestimated. But to regard spontaneous dialogues full of tension and conflict as useful requires a new awareness and set of skills on the part of teachers. As teachers, we must prepare ourselves to understand better the cultural and pedagogical dynamics involved in sound education in a multicultural society.

We need to prepare ourselves and our students to use such moments constructively. We need to anticipate what types of courses are likely to trigger such discussions and be willing to establish guidelines and provide useful information ahead of time to minimize unnecessary tension and hurt. As Beverly Tatum says about the use of information on racial identity development:

> Sharing the model of racial identity development with students gives them a useful framework for understanding each other's processes as well as their own. This cognitive framework does not necessarily prevent the collision of developmental processes . . . , but it does allow students to be less frightened by it when it occurs. . . . For instructors teaching courses with race-related content in other fields, it may seem less natural to do so. However, the inclusion of articles on racial identity development and/or class discussion of these issues . . . [can be] a very useful investment of class time. (1992, pp. 19–20)

We must respect such dialogues as an additional text which emerges alongside the text that was the intended focus of the class, a text deserving time and attention of its own. It may well end up being *the* significant text of the day—more influential than the intended text because of the immediacy and relevance of its focus and the level of personal and passionate involvement it evokes. We need to allow it to come into being. We need to recognize it and support it as the substantive exploration of life that it is. As one student said to me as this discussion unfolded, "There's so much anger here. You want to shut it off and go back to 'what we're supposed to do.' Let us talk. This is more important."

We have to know how to work with this discussion-as-text as it unfolds—how to interact with it, when to intervene, and when to allow it to take its course in the hands of the students. When to savor, when to question. We have to know how to interpret it and reflect on it, and be able to help our students do the same. Each discussion yields its own substance. Each must be read individually for what it can teach us: What can it teach of adolescent lives and needs today? What does it say of the human condition, of the strains that divide us, the humanity we share? We must accept that we will not have the answers our students seek, the control we might wish for, or the resolution that would comfort. The more we can help them understand these volatile discussions-as-texts, the more they can illuminate our lives.

We have to prepare our students to understand conflict in a multicultural society, to negotiate as it emerges, and to harness it for good rather than destruction. As Appleton suggests, [It is naive to think that] "understanding, respect, and toleration will lead to love and harmony among different groups" (1983, p. 234). But we can help students to learn about the sources, nature, and types of conflict natural in a pluralistic society; to understand their responses to it; and to engage in "constant and accurate communication" to reduce the inner and outer stresses produced by cultural conflict (Appleton, p. 232).

IMPLICATIONS BEYOND THE CLASSROOM

The dialogue as text has implications beyond the school as well.

Just as texts often reflect the eras that produce them, these discussions reveal the climate of the larger culture. They are indices of our workings as a people and the challenges that face us. Issues of race and culture are paramount in many students' minds. They are the substance of significant experiences in their lives, they are closely linked to their identity, and to their relationships with their peers. Although many today are quick to condemn such consciousness as "balkanization," these students' observations and behaviors are only painful reminders that it is we adults and our forefathers—not the young today—who through the years decided to create artificial divisions and privilege based on race and culture. We are reaping what we sowed.

As Toni Morrison has explained in speaking of her work, it is the duty of artists to help us remember our "disremembered" pasts (Benson, 1987). In the burdens they carry, the students in these discussions remind us not only of significant pasts that are still affecting daily lives, they remind us of the types of futures we are in the process of constructing.

The students need to engage in these discussions and we, the larger culture, need them to do so. The moments students choose to expose in such discussions indicate they are looking for help with navigating cultural seas full of threats and turbulence. They yearn to understand more about the histories and cultures of each other and the bearing that has on what they witness and experience in their daily lives. The prevalence of hate crimes around the nation reminds us that tensions in multicultural settings are widespread and persistent. There could be few better places to siphon off those tensions and examine their meanings than in a classroom. These discussions are the very stuff of education for life. Through them students can come to understand that some conflict is natural as we work out our notions of ourselves and each other and our lives in this society. And they see the role and limitations of dialogues as a crucial tool in that process. They see the inextricable link between the personal and the political, the private and the communal. The practice students gain in engaging in constructive dialogues across racial and cultural lines and in mediating the misunderstandings and tensions those moments produce benefit us all as these students move forward onto university campuses and into the workplaces of the future. As Linda Levine suggests, "What occurs in our classrooms on a daily basis . . . has ethical as well as political consequences for the future of this society" (1993, p. 91). And, fortunately or unfortunately, they see firsthand the strains and weaknesses that still characterize this long-running experiment in democracy.

It is instructive for all of us to realize the difficulty of engaging in public cross-cultural discussions. The personal, emotional, and sensitive nature of the issues, the diverging perspectives, the lack of models for the process, the lack of experience and skills the students have in engaging in them, the lack of ready language, the difficulty of expressing oneself clearly, and the ease of misunderstanding all hobble early attempts at creating smooth and constructive conversation on these issues. Such dialogues are often fast-moving and full of loose cannons; the impact of some spontaneous or even well-thought-out observations can never be undone. It is also important for us to know that in spite of the significant challenges in doing so, in spite of their individual vulnerability, and in spite of the toll it takes at times on group cohesiveness, these students are eager to engage in these discussions with each other, to listen to each other, and to confront thoughtfully together these difficult issues.

However hidden away in classrooms across the country, these dialogues are an American story—singly the students' own, together our own—and we had best be attentive. As Gustave Flaubert might say, *"Les dialogues. C'est nous."* And as Flannery O'Connor has said, "It requires considerable courage at any time, in any country, not to turn away from the storyteller" (Fitzgerald & Fitzgerald, 1969, p. 35).

Lastly, there are the hopes we have for our schools. "Schools have often been thought of as the vehicle for solving or resolving the ills of society . . . ," says Appleton. "Schools [are] an extremely important institution in our social response to cultural conflict. Because of their importance in the development and reinforcement of values, belief, and knowledge, schools have the potential to play an important role in the development, management, and understanding of cultural conflict" (1983, pp. 217–218). At the turn of the century, Dewey felt that schools were the crucible through which children from diverse backgrounds would be drawn to forge a more unified community of adults (1944). Many others had the same hope decades later, in the wake of *Brown v. Board of Education*. But that goal still eludes us. According to one recent report by Harvard University, (even) school integration is "virtually nonexistent" in the big cities (Grossman, Kirby, Leroux, & Thomas, 1994, p. 12). Within what mixed school communities we do have, students largely self-segregate. We continue to lead separate lives in this heterogeneous nation. Classes which do bring together students from multiple cultures offer a special challenge—in the innumerable divergences that accompany students into class—as well as special promise. The students and many of those of us who work with them continue to believe that education can and does make a difference in the way we ultimately relate to each other and live our lives.

These dialogues, then, reflect multiple facets of our relationship with our schools: the continued idealization of the role of schools in addressing cultural divisiveness, and the belief in dialogues as central to that process; the disillusionment students and educators alike experience as we live with the discrepancy between our notion of ourselves as ideal school or national community and the social realities of those communities; and the reparation we engage in every day, the hopes we hold onto, as we take ourselves back to school, back to class, and back to dialogues to try again to bring ourselves closer to living well together.

CONCLUSION

As I prepare class the day after the volatile discussion erupts, I decide the following: in an effort to begin to address some of the tensions of the preceding day, on the board I will write Paul Berman's words from a recent article in *The New Yorker* on cultural tensions: "The American Jews and the African-Americans are who they are because of long centuries of a past that can be put to different uses but cannot be overcome. It was the past that made the blacks and the Jews almost the same, and the past has the singular inconvenience of never going away" (1994, p. 71).

And in an effort at closure, I will turn to the students: "This week, an Eastern European, Jews, Blacks, and an Asian student talked about significant issues with each other. It has been hard. Together we have formidable pasts and presents to come to terms with. You were willing to talk about that. That seems important. If this country is going to work, that's what we have to be able to do and to keep doing it." I too keep hoping for reparation.

But that was a fantasy. In fact, I am afraid to reopen the cauldron so soon.

Instead, I turn directly to the text we were to examine the day the class exploded—Cynthia Ozick's "The Shawl" (1986), the story of a mother who attempts, against all odds, to keep two children alive in a concentration camp, where guards wait to hurl her daughter against an electrified fence. The conversation afterward is subdued. We are all still haunted by the text of the talking and its implications.

CHAPTER 4

WHAT WE LEARNED IN SCHOOL TODAY

Teaching Issues of Race and Culture

The Southern Poverty Law Center distributes free of charge to schools across the country close to 600,000 copies of a magazine called *Teaching Tolerance.* Oprah Winfrey hosts a benefit for Facing History, a case study approach to history that invites students to look at social issues today. Anna Deavere Smith's theater piece on the Los Angeles riots, *Twilight: Los Angeles, 1992* (1994), is nominated for a Tony Award. Incidents of hate crimes and racial violence escalate in communities and on campuses throughout the country. A college professor is "sentenced" to sensitivity training for the manner in which he addresses a student. And a fear of political incorrectness akin to the fear that swept campuses in the McCarthyism of the 1950s threatens ironically to promote intolerance in the very settings where the bid for tolerance heralded in the education movement known as multiculturalism. Tensions and bloodshed in our cities and schools are prompting us as a nation and particularly as educators to find ways to address the cultural divides and divisiveness that threaten our national unity. Is it possible, in our courses, to address directly these issues of race and culture? If so, how? What are the approaches, the pedagogy, the materials, the pitfalls?

One course focusing on these crucial issues has evolved at a hundred-year-old urban private progressive high school serving students from a wide range of socioeconomic backgrounds. Issues of Race and Culture is a team-taught one-semester interdisciplinary elective open to juniors and seniors for history or English credit. Now entering its eighth year, the course reveals compelling reasons why we as educators must address directly the cultural issues that surround our students. In many ways the course could be regarded as a model for exploring the issues, but it also underscores the challenges and difficulties of doing so.

The course examines lives and issues of Native Americans, African Americans, Jewish Americans, Asian Americans, and Latinos through the works of historians, cultural anthropologists, sociologists, psychologists, poets, short story writers, novelists, and filmmakers. The works studied explore issues the students are wrestling with in their own lives and are assembled to represent never a single perspective, but a number of the opposing perspectives which have made the issues so difficult to resolve. The novels represent some of the nation's best and most demanding writers and provide windows onto communities across the country by members of those communities. They also reveal the grace and resilience of the human spirit under sometimes intolerable conditions. At the end of the course, students opt to take a traditional exam or to design a public project based on an issue of race or culture. A glimpse into several classes as the course unfolds reveals not only the sometimes dazzling moments such courses can provide, but also the great difficulties in teaching about these issues as they engage both the mind and the heart.

The team-taught nature of the course has allowed my colleague, the chairman of the history department, and me to observe and to begin to understand multiple aspects of cross-cultural teaching and learning. Our students know we will be learning along with them, our queries will occur alongside theirs.

COMING TOGETHER

"Why do White supremacists think the way they do?"

"I'm Jewish, and I find that people—especially Blacks—tell me that I can never understand what they went through. Not only does this shut down conversation, it demeans both of us. I was never in a concentration camp, just as they were never in shackles, but we both have that in our past, so why shouldn't we try to talk about it instead of being abrupt?"

"I'm confused about equality and affirmative action: why must there be affirmative action if there is equality as a goal? Does affirmative action level or tilt the playing field?"

On the opening day of the course, students briefly describe issues of race or culture that trouble them. Several themes emerge: living with their own and each other's histories; coming to terms with racial or cultural identities and divisions; and understanding the reasons for stereotypes, prejudice, discrimination, and racism, and the thinking behind assimilation, integration, separatism, and quotas. Hearing such concerns allows us to know exactly which issues the students are confronting. The day closes with a video called "Race and Racism: Red, White, and Black" (Weinberg, 1991), an MTV-paced montage of individuals discussing issues from widely divergent points of view. The video immediately thrusts us as a group into the harshness of the issues that divide us, as well as the sweeping nature of these concerns across the country. We will begin the next day with students discussing specific lines that have particularly disturbed or moved them.

In the classes that follow, other introductory pieces include John Hope Franklin's concept of "the land of room enough" (1981), Robert Coles's work on the dreams of children of color (1981), and models illustrating the intimate relationship between history and literature, all of which lay a foundation for future explorations. We also establish the framework for the type of discussions we know will unfold in this course. Crucial in this process is reminding students that all of us come to the class with personal histories that have shaped our current perspectives, and that those perspectives are still evolving. If we are to explore the issues, we must be honest with each other, but also sensitive to each other's feelings and points of view as the discussions unfold.

We also introduce "seminaring," a seminar structure that allows students to discuss controversial, multifaceted, and personally involving topics in a manner that invites each person's voice and contribution, even as it subjects each perspective to scrutiny by the group. Before making his own observation, a student summarizes the previous observation, naming the contributor by name. Then, after offering his own point of view, he selects the next student to further the discussion. The process underscores the need to express one's ideas clearly, to listen carefully, and to try to understand others accurately. Multiple perspectives—and the challenges to those perspectives—come to life in front of us. And in the face of divisive issues, we weave, however tenuously or momentarily, a web of connectedness. Acting as guides, we teachers initiate questions, and, if the students are unable to resolve confusion or controversy on their own, offer additional information. The process is not easy. Students lack initially the role models, the model of a process, the language, the experience, and the skills with which to talk about differences. Regularly in these seminars, however, we are moved by these students' thinking, their interest in reaching across divides, their compelling need to understand each other, and their yearning to do what they feel is humane.

This year, one of the introductory works proves pivotal. The work is a small booklet called "Cultural Etiquette: A Guide for the Well Intentioned" (1991) by Amoja Three Rivers, a feminist of color. Throughout, the author calls on White readers to understand the effects of their often offhand though loaded gestures or remarks on people of color. Although we are expecting students to respond with cries of "political correctness" or to be sympathetic to the author's perspective, what unfolds is the first of a series of unusually intense and complicated seminars on key issues. Responding to Ms. Three Rivers's description of disrespectful ways in which Whites have responded to the hair of Black women, one young White male exclaims, "This could never happen on the streets here." Or as another White male explains, "She's incredibly angry. She's just ranting, and it's kind of scary." But for one young Black woman, the text has a much different effect: "Some of you have said, 'Why say all that about hair?' But [what Ms. Three Rivers describes] happens: I've had people, complete strangers, walk up to me and say [things about my hair and want to touch it]. A lot of you are offended by this book, but this is just bringing all of this out in the open—what some people have experienced in their life. People *have* gone through it. Learn from that. Don't take it offensively."

Dividing along cultural and racial lines, White students are unable to fathom that the cultural affronts described by the author can occur on the sophisticated streets of their city and are insulted to be seen simply as (offending) Whites. But many students of color, immediately identifying with the author, explain that she is merely describing the way things are. Within moments, it has become uncomfortably clear to White students what it feels like to be prejudged, stereotyped, and found lacking solely on the basis of one's racial identity. And many students of color have their perspective on the countless daily cultural misunderstandings and insults that intrude into their lives verified. As one student of color said of the usefulness of such texts, "If you know what offends me, it will make it easier for us to get along." Ms. Three Rivers's ideas will continue to haunt us in the coming weeks.

TEACHING ACROSS CULTURES

Classes next turn to issues of Native Americans. For our students, issues of Native Americans tend to be more removed, since our population is usually composed of Whites, Blacks, Latinos, and Asian Americans, with 20 to 25 percent students of color. But beginning with Native American issues allows us to construct a background of several paradoxical and significant aspects of the relationship between the dominant population and populations of color in this country. And precisely because a number of Native American issues are more removed from their own experiences, the students can gain practice in talking about sensitive, volatile issues before they address the issues more closely related to their own lives. A Michael Dorris article on Federal Indian policy (1981), a Pueblo Indian's childhood memories of a BIA boarding school (Suina, 1991), Jo Whitehorse Cochran's poem about a halfbreed girl in an urban school (1991), and *Powwow Highway* (Wacks, 1989), a film about the diverging paths taken by several young Native Americans, are placed beside Leslie Marmon Silko's novel *Ceremony* (1977).

Coming at the end of the first segment of the course, Silko's novel follows the return from World War II of a young Laguna Pueblo boy, shellshocked and war-sick. Only reconnection with the healing rituals of his own culture can soothe his wounds of war. The work is difficult, weaving together nonchronologically strands of history, contemporary social problems, and centuries-old rituals and ceremonies. Eager to help the students understand one of the central rituals of the novel, I decide to demonstrate, in skeletal fashion, a sand painting.

Gathering vials of colored sand and a large white roll of paper, I practice at home the evening before, rereading several times the description of Old Betonie's ritual to gain a better idea of the images. Although I've taught the novel before, I'm still searching for the best way to approach it—one that clarifies difficult and unfamiliar aspects of the novel but also allows the students to make significant connections themselves.

As class begins the next day, I explain that we will explore more fully one of the key rituals of the novel in order to understand not only the remaining experiences of the young man but the central political thrust of the novel. Simultaneously, I explain, I have serious reservations about what we are about to do. I explain the highly sacred nature of this and other rituals and explain that as with other Native American ceremonies, aspects of sand painting have moved, over the years, from the sacred to the secular to the commercial (Douglas George, personal communication, 1991): today, sand paintings can be purchased by art collectors, or, for a few dollars in tourist shops. Further, in placing the ritual at the center of the novel, Silko is making the ritual not only public, but a key to understanding her points about Native-American culture. We will approach the demonstration in that spirit.

Laying the large white sheet of paper on the floor, I ask one student to take a seat at the center, another to begin reading aloud the passages from the novel. As she reads, I sprinkle sand over the paper in the pattern Silko describes, explaining as I go the meaning of directions, colors, and patterns in the Navajo cosmology. The demonstration takes us to the end of the class. For the next class, we will conclude the novel, following the main character Tayo on his vision quest, into the mountains, deeper into his culture, toward home and healing.

A few moments after I return to my office, several students come by. "A couple of us were really bothered by what you did. It was a farce. It was a sacrilege . . . how could you do that—especially after what we talked about with 'Cultural Etiquette'?" We talk at length. I tell them to write down all their thoughts and say that their ideas will be the focus of the next class.

Part of me is stunned, part of me is intrigued. I have spent hours wrestling with how best to open this difficult and magnificent text for the students who are so far removed from this cosmology. I speak with colleagues, and that evening, my husband, a playwright and director. Although I can intellectualize the discomfort on some level, I feel I have failed, made a colossal public blunder in exactly the area we seek to address in the course—cross-cultural knowledge and sensitivity. I'm left with the ongoing uncertainty and frustration of trying to understand how best to do this kind of teaching. Was the demonstration an elaboration or violation? Did I violate cultural etiquette? My husband's take is different: "If I produce a play that's controversial, I feel I have succeeded. I wake up an audience, engage them. What about paintings of the crucifixion? What about the sacredness and rituals at the heart of Greek drama?"

The next day, I begin class by explaining that I understand several students were disturbed by the demonstration, that the course can work only if we are able to wrestle openly with the issues, and I would like to turn it over to the students to explain their concerns. For the next 70 minutes, the students seminar among themselves the vagaries of the demonstration and the manner in which we can learn of other cultures. Unflagging, they move through key issues. How can we teach and learn about others? Who can be an authority? What is offensive? How do we deal with the spiritual across cultures? Didn't the first anthropologist invited to view the ritual violate the sacred—or the photographer who gave us published images of a healer sprinkling the sand? How can we understand the unfamiliar?

By the end, I am both exhilarated and more challenged. I feel a nagging discomfort at having walked through a minefield. On the one hand, the conversation confirms the challenges I have articulated elsewhere that await the White teacher in teaching texts by writers of color (Dilg, 1995). On the other hand, the class has generated a seminar worthy of these tough issues: multiple perspectives come to light, the complexities laid bare in front of us. And we leave it unresolved. But our students have been passionately and thoughtfully engaged in debating issues that continually haunt us as we try to live together and understand each other in our multicultural communities.

A few days later, in a chance for more private reflection, the students submit writings about rituals in their own lives. They are exquisite: evocations of a secular springtime sowing of seeds by mother and daughter, now coming to an end as the child readies for college; Memorial Day plantings at a cemetery and a remembering of those who have died; biannual national family reunions with elders recalling how their ancestors survived slavery.

There is, however, a postscript to this segment of the course.

Months later, and still haunted by questions surrounding the use of the sand painting in class, I enroll in a course called "Art and the Healing Process Rooted in Native-American Tradition," at Ghost Ranch in Abiquiu, New Mexico. The course is co-taught by a Blackfoot Indian artist and an Anglo art historian who has spent years teaching young Native Americans from multiple tribes in the Southwest. The course examines the relationship between art and Native-American healing rituals. By week's end, we have taken part in two healing ceremonies and heard the teachings of a Santa Clara herbalist and a Navajo weaver.

Near the end of the course I ask one of the instructors about my decision the previous fall to offer a quasi-demonstration of a sand painting. We talk at length about the challenges of cross-cultural teaching, and in her answer, I find the clarity I have been seeking. In her opinion, I had indeed violated the spirit of the sand painting. Similarly to my students, the art historian explains that as Anglos we are unable, ultimately, to understand the ritual as a Navajo would. And as a number of my students had suggested months before, the demonstration had been a form of sacrilege, akin to taking on the role of a priest and demonstrating the offering of communion. The ritual had been taken out of its proper context and offered by an individual not properly initiated into the sacred tradition it represents. "It's real problematic," the art historian says, "even with good intent" (Joy Gritton, personal communication, July 1994).

More than a thousand miles from home, under cottonwood trees overlooking the flat-topped mountain called the Pedernal, I realize that my own disconnectedness from any form of spirituality or sacred rituals led me stumbling into an area I could little understand and even less fully appreciate. Unlike my more spiritually sensitive students, and eager to wed an artistically and intellectually intricate ritual with the experiential pedagogy of Dewey, I had erred in a significant and public way. To approach these writers and issues, we must rely not only on the mind and the heart, but also on the promptings and wisdom of the soul.

Today, the vials of brightly colored sand I had gathered to teach Silko's novel line the back of my desk—a reminder of the complexities of this kind of teaching and of how much I have to learn. As I approach the novel now, I rely on anthropologists' descriptions and illustrations to convey the intricacies of sand painting to my students. And memories of the controversy surrounding my original choice of using a demonstration become part of the conversations the students and I share—whether about the novel, or about the difficulty of learning about each other and each other's worlds.

LEARNING AND LIVING WITH HISTORIES

Within a few weeks we are once again in the midst of the challenges that simultaneously enthrall us and remind us of the profoundly difficult tasks we face not only as educators but as a multicultural nation. In the African-American section of the course, several chapters from Genovese's writing on the slave culture (1974); articles on peer pressure among black students (Gregory, 1992) and race on campus (Barnet, 1991; Jacoby, 1991; Steele, 1989; Weisberg, 1991); a documentary on Malcolm X (*Malcolm X*); an excerpt of Louis Farrakhan speaking to the Congressional Black Caucus; Jefferson Morley's "Rap Music as American History" (1992) and rappers on MTV; several opposing texts on affirmative action (Dudley, 1991); and Marlon Riggs's films *Ethic Notions* (1987) and *Color Adjustment* (Kleiman & Riggs, 1991) are placed beside Toni Morrison's exploration of a black community in Ohio in *Sula* (1973).

Initially, as we were designing the course, our thought that the Holocaust and Jewish-American writers were covered in other courses led us to focus primarily on issues affecting other cultures. Each year, however, discussions of African-American issues resulted in comparisons between slavery and the Holocaust, and between racism and anti-Semitism. This year, with Black-Jewish relations at the heart of an ongoing national debate, and knowing the tensions that exist among our own students, we decide to focus directly on the Black-

Jewish dialogue. Beginning with viewing *Fires in the Mirror* (1993), Anna Deavere Smith's theater piece on Black-Jewish conflicts in the Crown Heights section of Brooklyn, students are also asked to consider Cornel West's perspective on Black-Jewish relations in *Race Matters* (1993), and Bernard Malamud's short story "Black Is My Favorite Color" (1983), about an aging Jewish merchant in Harlem who falls in love with a Black woman. Even we are unprepared for the discussion that follows this trio of perspectives.

The ensuing seminar reveals to us not only the confusion and pain that sometimes divide these students and their cultures, but also a kind of structural paradigm that emerges in discussions of issues which are so emotionally laden.

What we witness is an emotional outpouring of histories: Black and Jewish students releasing the pressure of years of living with bitter histories, losses, and resentments. An intensity of debate like sobbing emerges, a pouring forth of group and personal stories of mistreatment, dislocated lives, and deaths. Once again, the students' remarks establish a competition of historical brutalities and present indignities, each student so yearning to have the wounds of his own culture tended that it is difficult, especially for adolescents still coming to terms with their own identities and histories, to acknowledge the pain of others. As a group, we wrestle with the nature of evil and discuss whether evil has degrees, whether one can compare historical brutalities and sweeping horrors, how we can live with and address these histories, and where we can go from here. As the discussion unfolds, a pattern emerges: first, the sobbing intensity, the need to release years of frustration, hurt, and anger, the need to place the stories before us. Story upon story of individual lives vie for understanding, for recognition—understand me, understand my history, help me:

> [The Black man in the video] said you can't compare slavery and the Holocaust because slavery lasted 300 years. That offended me. It made a mockery of the Holocaust.
>
> Jews chose to come here and kept their culture, but African Americans were stripped of their culture and not allowed to express it.
>
> The Jews had to leave, too—or be thrown into concentration camps. A lot *were* stripped of their culture.
>
> Leah's grandparents were in a concentration camp. Her grandmother watched two children walk into a building and die.
>
> Jews are White so they're accepted more.
>
> There are a lot of Jewish jokes: "Throw a penny and see who the Jews are." I don't think it's funny.

Then, a need to strike out. What these students really want to hit are forces larger than any of us, but this they cannot do. And so they attack whatever is near: the use of the personal, the course, even the seminaring structure that has guided and sustained us:

Stay off the personal!
You shot his comment down just because he didn't remember to sum up the earlier point!

But gradually we witness the subsiding of intensity, of the intellectual sobbing, the need to attack. Somehow, the open attacks on aspects of the discussion help them, and the debate takes a final turn:

We should take advantage of what this course is giving us. We can learn about each other's backgrounds.

This understanding, this clarity, the need for reparation, produces in the end a sense of relative calm.

A few days later, after screening a video on hate hosted by Bill Moyers (Tatge & Lasseur, 1992), my teaching partner and I are preparing to leave the room. We see two young Black women and two young Jewish women talking. They have decided to do their final project together—designing a course on genocides in history, something they feel would educate students about each other, and in that, foster understanding. We hear one of them say, "Remember the video talking about reconciliation. That's what's important."

Based on what we have seen this year, we will restructure the course to create a section on Jewish Americans. *Maus* (Spiegelman, 1991), which focuses on the personal horrors at the heart of the Holocaust, will be placed beside *Beloved* (1987), Morrison's dazzling exploration of slavery, to enable students to explore seminal experiences in both Black and Jewish histories. To our trio on the Black-Jewish dialogues we will add a major article by Paul Berman in *The New Yorker* called "The Other and the Almost the Same" (1994). Through these perspectives, we will explore what some have called the "bridges and boundaries" between these two cultures that have much in common and yet at times are so divided.

VISITING LIVES

The section on Asian Americans opens with a panel of Japanese Americans discussing the internment of their families during World War II and the screening of *Days of Waiting* (Okazaki, 1990), a documentary about one woman's experiences at the Heart Mountain detention center. One of the panelists speaks not only of the internment but also of his work leading the national fight for reparations. Another panelist describes the impact of those years on her identity:

I lived with this mystery about who I was. I didn't come to terms with [the internment] until I was an adult. I was ashamed of being Japanese-American because it was never explained why we were put in the camps. . . . None of my classmates could talk to me about it. When I see this kind of course where you can talk openly about these issues, it's gratifying to me. We never had this opportunity.

Articles in this section of the course focus on "the new look of affirmative action," the charge of quotas at West Coast universities (Hacker, 1989), and the realities behind the stereotype of the "model minority" (Suzuki, 1989). The film *Eat a Bowl of Tea* (Sternberg, 1989) and Amy Tan's novel *The Joy Luck Club* (1989) take us, respectively, into the lives of families coping with the effects of the Exclusion Acts and with the challenges of immigration. Although Tan's novel is both compelling storytelling and a complex look at cultural issues, I wondered initially if it would resonate for young men in the class, since it focuses primarily on mothers and daughters. Each year, however, beyond the following it finds among young women, the novel has had some of its greatest successes with children of cross-cultural marriages and with young men. As one young man leaving the class said this year, "You'll never find a better book than this, Ms. D., never."

The last two weeks of the course focus on Latino issues. We establish a historical framework which examines the status of persons and property included in the United States after the Treaty of Guadalupe Hidalgo. An article by Carlos Arce helps us look at issues of Chicano identity (1981), the film *El Norte* (Thomas, 1984) offers us images of immigration, a video of a Latino comedy company raises questions about the relationship between culture and humor, and selected poetry and scenes from *West Side Story* (Wise & Robbins, 1997) allow us to explore Latino stereotypes. With Rolando Hinojosa's *This Migrant Earth* (1987) and Sandra Cisneros's *The House on Mango Street* (1989), we travel into rural and urban Chicano communities and issues of immigration, housing, employment, language, identity, history, and memory.

Our last visitors are two activists from the local Puerto Rican community. They enter the room carrying a twenty-foot mural on Puerto Rican history done by youths in the community. They open with a brief history lesson on Puerto Rico from early influences up through the vote on statehood and how that affects Puerto Ricans living here. The other issue they share concerns the attempt by community leaders to place a statue of Puerto Rican patriot Dr. Pedro Albizu Campos in a local park. They describe his life, his heroic stature to many, and the obstacles they encounter in the city bureaucracy. The sculptor works in natural material—resin. For the park, a statue must be bronze. Another rejection, another hurdle, another fund-raising. Students sit on the floor looking up enrapt at these women who dare, day by day, to take on the powers above them that shape and misshape their lives. Students ask about immigrating, about gentrification. These women, whose neighbors' lives have been displaced by those not unlike, socioeconomically, many of our students, bring home a visceral reality of what it means to recast a community, inching out generations who can no longer afford the rents. They promise to come again.

In the end, only one student opts to take an exam rather than to develop a public project. The projects allow students to clarify what has had meaning for them in the course and then to act responsibly on their convictions in ways that affect directly their own communities. The projects are varied and satisfying. Several students outline cultural sensitivities from Black and from Puerto Rican points of view in formal brochures for distribution within the school. Other students lead seminars on Toni Morrison; rap music; discrimination in sports; and the responsibility to one's community, during a teach-in on Martin Luther King Day. A young Black student who understands well many of the ironies of history gives a formal presentation to the student body based on a twenty-page paper he has written on "ghetto mentality." The young Black and Jewish women who have worked together present publicly the course design on genocides.

In most cases, however, despite the community orientation of the projects, their real meaning is probably more personal, and the real gains probably lie within the students themselves as they bring the projects into being. Early on, in the planning stages, the young women who designed the course on genocides had said to us, "It's for you. It's to say what it all meant."

WHAT WE'VE LEARNED

What does it all mean? These issues? These students searching us, and texts, and each other for answers, for some kind of understanding of the past and present? What has the course taught us? How can it serve as a model for addressing directly these issues of race and culture?

The success of the course in helping students address the issues rests on several key elements:

The course embodies some of the most basic principles of both progressive and multicultural education. The course comes from the students—their questions, their issues, their needs; the history and the literature of their cultures. Daily, the passionate conversations among students confirm what Dewey articulated long ago in *Experience and Education*: that problems are a stimulus to thought; that education should begin with the present experiences of the student; and that the exploration of those problems or experiences should heighten and deepen the students' curiosity and thinking (1963, p. 79).

The course is ever responsive to changing political and cultural conditions within the class, school, neighborhood, or nation, thus remaining focused on the students' need to understand their world. As a result, we teachers must remain abreast of current conditions which affect the students, abreast of the thinkers and artists who best address those conditions, and flexible enough to modify continually the structure and content of the course. Our own ongoing collaboration and our debriefings with each other result in our constantly re-shaping the course. Recent works by Ronald Takaki (1993) and Arthur Schlesinger (1992) are drawn in for opposing perspectives on cultural pluralism. The film version of William Styron's *Sophie's Choice* (Pakula & Barish, 1982), used in part to raise questions about insider and outsider perspectives in telling our stories, is replaced by Spiegelman's *Maus* (1991). *West Side Story* (Wise & Robbins, 1997), as a mirror of Latino stereotypes, gives way to narratives on Chicano lives in the era of affirmative action (Navarrette, 1993) and gangs (Rodriguez, 1993).

We also need to be able to help students link the kinds of understanding they gain from texts and discussions with actual events. When riots tore through South Central Los Angeles one night, the next morning we set aside our discussion of Amy Tan's novel and screened excerpts from *Nightline* to allow students to sort out their reactions to unfolding events. The next class, however, as we concluded our look at Asian-American literature, we turned to several poems. Just as the novelist and poets in front of us had created order and beauty from social and political chaos, we could contemplate that someday, artists would help us better understand the painful events exploding on the streets of Los Angeles.

The course blends elements of several discrete approaches to multicultural education. In a major analysis of multicultural education in the United States, Sleeter and Grant (1987) describe five specific approaches to multicultural curriculum design, several of which are apparent in the course. The "human relations" approach is reflected in: addressing the origins and effects of prejudice and racism; acquainting students with the histories, lives, and writers of diverse communities; and promoting understanding among the students. Our examining one specific culture at a time resembles "single group studies." And our emphasizing multiple cultures with none dominant evokes aspects of the "multicultural education" approach (1987, pp. 426–434). The course draws on other models as well. In its inclusion of texts that have the ability to extend or expand our perspectives beyond those of mainstream voices, it reflects Banks's "transformation" approach (1993a, pp. 203–204). And last, in its promotion of analytical and critical thinking about social constructs, and in the opportunity it affords students to put their ideas to work in public projects, it reflects elements of the "social reconstructionist" approach (Sleeter & Grant, 1987, pp. 434–436) or the "social action approach" (Banks, 1993a, pp. 205–206). As a whole, the course also reflects the use of what McIntosh describes as appropriate pedagogy and sources of knowledge for this type of study. The course explores numerous cultures through the daily lives, testimonies, and arts that are part of those cultures; it relies on multiple works, media, perspectives, and voices, including the students' own; and it admits the attendant democratizing shift in pedagogy and authority (1990, pp. 5, 7, 11–12).

The pedagogy—which relies on the use of articles, works of literature, films, videos, speakers, and student-led discussions—acknowledges and respects a variety of ways of knowing: facility with the abstract, the personal, the written, visual, and verbal. As such, the course is responsive to different learning styles, some of which are culturally influenced, and this allows students to capitalize on their own strengths as learners. The course rests solidly on cooperative learning and confirms research suggesting that cooperative, noncompetitive learning fosters positive interaction across racial and cultural lines (Aronson & Thibodeau, 1992, p. 245; Slavin, 1992, p. 345). Speakers from the students' own communities help minimize the discontinuity some students feel between their cultural life at home and the culture of the school (Appleton, 1983, p. 215) and help broaden the intercultural contact fostered in class discussions.

By our following the cues of our own students, the course has come to reflect many guidelines for effective multicultural education (Appleton, 1983, pp. 205–217; Banks, 1993a, pp. 210–212). In keeping with Appleton's suggestions for effective multicultural education, the course is constructed to take into consideration the students' own experiences and needs, to foster skills development as well as critical thinking, to use materials and resources that examine historical and contemporary social issues in the students' own communities, and to acknowledge the importance of affective as well as cognitive dimensions of teaching and learning (1983, pp. 205–217). Consistent with Banks's suggestions for sound multicultural education, we teachers attempt to be ever sensitive to our own racial attitudes; we engage in a careful selection of materials, and are especially mindful of including the perspectives of people of color; we use a variety of types of material—films, books, videos, and recordings; we are sensitive to the developmental levels of the students; and we employ cooperative learning techniques (Banks, 1993a, pp. 210–212). Perhaps most important, we attempt to help our students "to know, to care, and to act in ways that will develop and foster a democratic and just society . . . " (Banks, 1991, p. 140).

The reliance on seminaring results in a natural and significant distribution of authority, a democratizing of the classroom. In daily discussions, the "learned authority" of those who have spent years studying these issues is regularly equaled or surpassed in power and significance by the "lived authority" that comes from those whose lives and perspectives—including those of our students—have been affected directly by the issues.

In their 1987 analysis of multicultural education in the United States, Sleeter and Grant noted that while considerable work had been done to address the curriculum of multiculturalism, little had been done on pedagogy. Surely, the authors suggested, a multicultural approach would demand a new pedagogy, one which moved away from traditional teacher-dominated practices. Our experience confirms that a dispersal of authority is a powerful, naturally occurring, and appropriate phenomenon in the discussion of these issues; to deny or thwart it directly contradicts the concepts that are central to the course. Our own concepts of "learned" and "lived" authority correspond closely to what Banks has designated, respectively, as "mainstream" and "transformative academic" knowledge, and "personal and cultural knowledge" (1993b, pp. 6–11). The result of the decentralization of authority reflects what Appleton calls "democracy in action" (1983, p. 212) and the "dialogical approach of Paulo Freire" which, as Appleton suggests, increases "student-initiated dialogue and . . . stimulate[s] critical thinking" (1983, p. 213). It also embodies what McIntosh describes as a key aspect of "Curricular Re-Vision": "All voices count. Pedagogy shifts so that the professor's forms of knowing are not necessarily superior to the students' forms of knowing. . . . All experience is seen as a source of knowledge" (1990, p. 7).

The interdisciplinary nature of the course allows students the opportunity to see compelling thinkers and artists from a variety of disciplines address common concerns. Drawing on works from several disciplines allows students to see both the shared objectives of multiple disciplines and the distinctions that distinguish those disciplines. Historians and social scientists cannot bundle and tie off the loose ends of human experiences, and thus they leave us with the true and ragged edges of history. But the artist can offer us beauty, design, and closure, no matter how dark the human drama from which his story comes. At the end of the section on African Americans one year, we had turned to Andrew Hacker's bleak statistics on what he calls our "two nations" (1992). Although Hacker's vision allows, rightly, no comfortable reckoning, the next day we concluded our reading of Toni Morrison's novel *Sula* (1973), and there, amid the "circles and circles of sorrow" within those two nations, found beauty and closure.

As teachers we attempt to be cognizant of a wide array of factors emanating from the effect of cultural identities on the process of teaching and learning about these issues. Many texts and testimonies make clear that teaching across racial and cultural lines is associated with a host of challenges related to racial or cultural identities. As Michelle Foster so vividly explores in her work on Black teachers (1997), many Black families have reasons, deep-seated in history, to greet White teachers of their children with suspicion. In the aftermath of desegregation, Black teachers lost their jobs in great numbers as they were replaced by White teachers (Foster, 1997, p. xxxviii); and White teachers were known to have humiliated Black students, failed to understand their needs, and failed to hold them to high standards of achievement (Foster, 1997). Meanwhile, many Black families continued to fight for Black teachers for their children, and Black teachers were considered unsuitable to teach White students (1997, p. xxxi, p. xxviii). In separate commentaries spanning several generations, a Black teacher at the turn of the century, W. E. B. DuBois in 1935, and a Black teacher in California today all express concerns for the well-being of Black students being taught by White teachers (Foster, 1997). Fiction writers such as Leslie Marmon Silko (1977), Frank Chin (1991), and Hugo Martinez-Serros (1988) have used their novels and short stories to call attention to negative effects of White teachers on Native-American, Asian-American, and Latino students. Teachers of color repeatedly recall resistance on the part of White students to seeing them as legitimate figures of authority (Adams, Bell, & Griffin, 1997, p. 308). Anecdotal evidence abounds of students of color feeling uncomfortable in the classrooms of White teachers or White students feeling uneasy working with teachers of color—especially for reasons surrounding difficulty with communication and expectations. Such gaps are potentially deepened when teachers or students bring to the class overt political agendas. As the research on culturally influenced styles of learning continues to mount, White teachers and teachers of color have reason to assume they have much to learn to handle satisfactorily, teaching across the lines of cultural identities.

In any forum in which individuals consider issues of race and culture from multiple viewpoints, the cultural or racial identities of the individuals involved play a central, inescapable, fundamental role in the dialogue and are often a significant factor in shaping its thrust and its emotional tenor. Each individual's cultural identity, each individual's relationship to that identity and to the identities of others in the group, and each individual's stage in the development of his or her racial or cultural identity (Tatum, 1992) become salient aspects of the process of teaching and learning about these issues. As teachers and students come together as a group, the educational process continually involves an interplay of their cultural identities and backgrounds, as well as the biases, prejudices, values, or needs extending from those identities. The impact of cultural identities is complicated further when the educational process involves adolescents, since one of the central developmental tasks for adolescents is the creation of a stable identity and since an adolescent's sense of his or her identity is in flux, is often vulnerable, and is at times in turmoil. These factors shape the course and its dynamics in a number of ways.

As teachers, we acknowledge to ourselves and to students that cultural identities influence teaching and learning about these issues, and indeed, this becomes part of the focus of the course. As the course unfolds, we teachers attempt to be sensitive to the effects of our own cultural identities, backgrounds, educations, and values on the process of working with students with these issues. We are ever aware that our identities and social and political values determine in part what will and will not occur in a given class or in the course itself. As teachers, we attempt to create a forum through which students may feel free to explore and examine options unbiased by our biases. At the same time, we attempt to be candid about our biases or about the ways in which our identities may limit our own understanding or presentation of the issues. We attempt to limit the effect of our own perspectives by placing in the foreground the perspectives of scholars and artists from multiple cultures and the voices of the students themselves. Thus, as part of the educational process, we explore the ways in which individuals' perspectives are influenced—but not determined—by their identities, whether those individuals are scholars, artists, the students, or we ourselves.

We structure the course in ways that assure that our own perspectives as teachers—coming in part from our own identities—will be challenged or broadened by those of the scholars and artists whose works we include and by those of the students. To the extent that a single voice—whether it is that of a teacher, a scholar, an artist, or a student—attempts to drown out others, the open nature of the forum is lessened. What makes establishing a healthy flow of ideas doubly difficult, however, is deciding if or when a perspective is a destructive one—either for individuals or the group, or in the larger context of human rights—and who makes that determination and how, since that decision too will be influenced by factors related to individual identity.

We and the students must work to overcome the prejudices—in part linked to our identities—that accompany us to the group. The open and supportive nature of the forum depends in large part on the extent to which we teachers and the students are able to put aside actively our own destructive biases.

As teachers, we encourage an atmosphere of open questioning, and we understand that questions may well and indeed should, for the sake of broader exploration, be turned upon us and our choices. The process of teaching across lines of cultural identities becomes part of the focus of the inquiry; that is, the students may explore or scrutinize the joys and challenges inherent in that process. This makes for layers of learning, since students are learning about the process of teaching and learning as well as the subject matter of that teaching or learning. The result of such exploration led one young White woman to remark at the end of the course one year, "When I get a text now, I'm going to say: Who wrote this? What's being included and what's being left out? There's been this empty space that's been what's been left out of what was presented." Inherent in this young woman's observation is not only a critical examination of a text, but by extension, a questioning of the process by which the text was selected. Her observation suggests she is becoming a more active participant in her education. Her question is a question about power, authority, point of view, pedagogy, inclusion, and exclusion—as each relates, in part, to cultural identity.

As teachers, we must continually earn the students' respect or trust to work with them effectively with these issues. The degree to which we can address satisfactorily the challenges emanating from the interplay of cultural or racial identities within the group—including our own—will in large part determine the degree to which we can work successfully with these issues.

The course provides a focus and process for understanding self and others in both cognitive and affective manners. Regularly, students are able to see lives and experiences similar to their own in the articles, novels, and videos, and in the words of the guest speakers. They see national experts wrestle with the same concerns they share, and see members of their own cultures or communities as key spokespersons in influential positions making significant observations or decisions. Whether emerging from the Laguna Pueblo in the Southwest, a Black community in Ohio, a Jewish community in New York, Asian Americans in San Francisco, or Chicanos in Chicago, the novels focus on young people coming to terms with their identities, histories, and experiences embedded in multicultural America. The degree of the students' engagement in the works and discussions daily supports what Banks suggests in describing the relationship between student motivation and material: that students are more involved when curriculum reflects their own cultures and experiences (1993a, p. 195). And although discussions of these issues may easily stress group cohesiveness, far from creating the balkanization feared by many opponents of multiculturalism (Schlesinger, 1992), in our experience, the reliance on these texts encourages group relatedness and communication among our already culturally divided students.

In addition to focusing on their own cultures, the students also learn firsthand of the cultures and challenges of those around them, what Appleton refers to as a crucial "de-centering" (1983, p. 210), that is, moving beyond the examination of one's own culture to being able to see oneself as part of a larger interdependency among individuals from many different ethnic groups. As Appleton notes, such de-centering balances the study of one's own culture with a focus on the interconnectedness of lives across ethnic or racial lines. In our experience, for promoting such cross-cultural understanding there is no substitute for these students talking and listening to each other as they describe the impact of the issues on their own lives. In some moments that means learning of the pain that many of our students regularly endure—taunts, exclusion, police harassment. In other moments it means being privy to the coping strategies, compassion, wisdom, and complexity of thought so evident in these late adolescents.

Through the often passionate, often disturbing, and always multisided discussions, students come to see both the gulfs that separate and stress them as a group, and the overarching likenesses that invite them to come together. As Linda Levine has suggested, this can have far-reaching consequences. The school becomes a "public sphere" (Giroux, 1987, quoted in Levine, 1993, p. 88) where students and adults can engage in crucial "dialogue[s] across differences"

(Burbules & Rice, 1991, quoted in Levine, 1993, p. 88). This in turn can expand students' ability to communicate " . . . in ways that have enormous potential for improving social life in a multicultural society" (Levine, 1993, p. 97). Even the emotional dimension of such exchanges is significant. As Appleton explains, "feelings and emotions can be powerful stimulators of truly creative and meaningful learning experiences" (Jones, 1968, quoted in Appleton, 1983, pp. 213–214). "The affective dimension is especially important in learning about cultures different from one's own" (Appleton, 1983, p. 214).

The course allows students to develop a greater understanding of conflict, especially as it occurs naturally in pluralistic societies. The course is what Nicholas Appleton calls "conflict sensitive." In his excellent discussion of cultural conflict, Appleton suggests that such conflict is an ongoing, pervasive feature of life in a pluralistic society, and in fact, is at times an agent for productive change. To assume that one can educate conflict away in a society such as ours is not only naive, but erroneous. To educate students about conflict is important: its nature, origins, types, and functions in the lives of individuals and groups. Although we mustn't construe such a focus as advocating conflict as a mode of problem solving, the tendency to stay away from conflict and controversy, as do many schools and teachers, may do students a disservice; the avoidance or absence of conflict is not necessarily an index of community health (Appleton, 1983).

In this course, in the safe setting of a classroom, with the two of us ready to guide or diffuse passions, students not only examine conflict; they also at times experience it. The request for student concerns that opens the course invites areas of conflict from school or community life into the dialogues of the course, where tensions can be named, released, explored, and often, in the process, tamed. In readings and discussions, students examine the roots and impacts of conflict in their own or their classmates' cultures. And regularly, during discussions, we are privy to our students experiencing the personal and group conflicts involved as they come to terms with their own and each other's racial and cultural identities and values, conflicts which Appleton suggests are a natural and healthy part of the formation of those identities and values (1983).

The students also experience the usefulness as well as the limitations of dialogue in addressing those conflicts. While seminaring leads to relatively comfortable resolutions of feelings surrounding many issues for the group, there are also days when heated discussions spill out into the halls after class, and the conflictual nature of the discussions or the lack of resolution of feelings surrounding the conflict is still haunting the students when they return to class the next day. Such moments can be uncomfortable, both for students and teachers, but they also begin to prepare students realistically for their multicultural world.

In an excellent discussion of similar dynamics among very young schoolchildren, Linda Levine notes: "Almost daily, [there are moments] at which conflicting assumptions and worldviews underlying behavior become apparent in classroom discourse. . . . Too seldom are such moments viewed as opportunities for joint exploration and . . . as a stimulus for democratic public dialogue" (1993, p. 91). Proper mediating of these moments on the part of teachers "can do much to help children question and move beyond currently prevailing notions about dominant and subordinate cultures within the United States" (1993, p. 108). Often in the seminars in this course, students gain experience in engaging in dialogues about contentious issues, in understanding the importance of listening, and in tolerating multiple irreconcilable differences emanating from our pluralistic culture. They begin to learn to manage cultural conflict in a healthy and peaceful manner. In recognizing this ongoing effect of the course for the school community as a whole, the school's curriculum office has continued to offer financial support for course materials and has turned to the course seeking student leadership in shaping the school's annual, day-long teach-in marking Martin Luther King Day.

The course offers students ways of knowing or living with their past, present, and future. Although George Santayana has said that "those who cannot remember the past are condemned to repeat it" (1980, p. 284), experience has shown us that it is often the memory of the past that places a burden on these students. They live not only with the injustices in those pasts, but also with the insensitivity or ignorance about those pasts on the part of those around them. Materials throughout the course focus on the pasts of each culture considered and the effects of those pasts on all of us today.

Through seminaring, students begin to talk about the uncertainties, the tensions, and the questions that simmer amid and around them, day to day. They begin to understand the origins and the real meanings and effects of prejudice, racism, discrimination, and stereotypes. They begin to be able to talk with each other about each other's lives and needs.

And as they examine and begin to formulate opinions on issues that will increasingly affect their lives—affirmative action or quotas in college admissions; political correctness, separatism, and hate crimes on university campuses; employment and housing practices; and what Ellis Cose has termed "the rage of a privileged class" (1993)—they begin to understand something of their futures.

The course offers students tools not only for understanding, but for action. In our experience, the more students understand the issues, the more they want to take thoughtful action in relation to them. The projects at the end of the course allow them to use their knowledge to engage in direct action in the community. In this manner they experience the satisfaction of acting responsibly on their beliefs and of seeing themselves as agents for productive change. While the experience of taking an exam is private, individualistic, competitive, and theoretical, the projects are public, communal, cooperative, and concrete, and thus more consistent with the goals of community-mindedness.

As teachers we attempt to model for our students an active engagement with racial and cultural issues, especially as they impact on education. Ideals articulated by Progressive educators earlier in the century, as well as the work of a number of contemporary multiculturalists, suggest that education about these issues might logically be tied to community activism. One has only to recall the tireless work of Jane Addams in social reform or to note the emphasis on social action advocated by multiculturalists such as James Banks (1993a, pp. 205–206). Thus far, for us as teachers, our primary concern has been and continues to be addressing the needs of students—whether in creating the focus for the course, selecting the materials we will use, or designing the pedagogy we will employ. Through our work with the students, through our related work on curriculum and pedagogy, and through our research on relevant social and educational issues, we continue to educate ourselves about cross-cultural teaching and learning in order to better address and serve the needs of the students.

As teachers, and at times with our students, however, we reach out to the parents and to the larger community in a number of ways. We invite parent involvement with our work through a variety of formats. A fall open house enables parents to hear about the focus and structure of the course. Parents are invited to join us for classes at any time—as guests or as speakers—to share their perspectives or concerns. And although parents have not taken a direct role in planning the course, our listening to parents continually affects and directs our thinking and our planning. Perhaps because many parents believe the course reflects a commitment within the school to addressing crucial issues with students, there has been ongoing support for the course among White parents and parents of color. Additionally, through speaking at evening programs for parents, accepting invitations to speak at other schools, speaking at regional or national conferences, and through publishing our work in journals and magazines, we have attempted to support the needs and wishes of families in the community, to encourage dialogues about issues in multicultural education, and to educate colleagues, other professionals, and members of the community at large about the challenges and benefits of teaching and learning informed by a multicultural awareness.

In a reciprocal manner, each of these engagements educates us further. Hearing from parents, community leaders, educators, psychologists, and social workers enables us to track community concerns and to continually reshape our work in response to an ever broader understanding of the issues surrounding this form of education and the needs of students and their families.

THE CHALLENGES FOR TEACHERS

Despite the success of the course for students and the pleasure it gives us as educators, to enjoy and to thrive in courses such as this places special demands on teachers.

1. Teachers must be willing to engage in preparation which is extensive, ongoing, and responsive to changing social and political conditions, especially in compensating for the monoculturalism of their own academic backgrounds.
2. They must be able to tolerate and mediate the natural personal and group conflicts that emerge in discussions.
3. Even if they are skilled moderators, they must be able to manage, and learn ways of helping students manage, unpredictability in the direction, tone, and outcome of observations and discussions.
4. They must be able to create a classroom climate that simultaneously encourages honesty, trust, respect, support, and empathy.
5. They must be willing to see themselves as resource and guide; they must be willing to experiment with new materials and approaches, to share their power and authority, and to make mistakes and know and acknowledge they have made them.
6. They must be able to be self-critical, to know they will not always have answers, and, in the spirit of fostering sound critical inquiry, to be as willing as their students to have their assumptions and observations questioned.
7. They must attempt to be sensitive and responsive to each student's affective and cognitive needs as those needs emerge from multiple cultural and socioeconomic factors, and they must be constantly alert to the ways in which their own biases or lack of knowledge affect their curricular and pedagogical decisions.
8. They must be able to tolerate the discouragement that comes with knowing the limitations of schooling in addressing sweeping social phenomena—that is, to savor the joys and gains from this kind of teaching and to tolerate the limitations.
9. They must be prepared for the fact that their work may be controversial. The pedagogy of multiculturalism is often misunderstood. Diane Ravitch suggests that multiculturalism is merely an extension of the egos of those with political agendas of their own (Edwards, 1993, p. 13). But our experience suggests that pedagogy grounded in multiple cultures demands and exacts an extraordinary degree of humility. Dinesh D'Souza and Alan Bloom have contended that the pedagogy of multiculturalism is associated with an "illiberal education," and "a tyranny of the minority" (D'Souza, 1991), or a "closing of the mind" (Bloom, 1987). But experience has shown us that constructing educations consistent with the essential identity and

values of this country is associated with pedagogical skills and sensibilities sweepingly broader and more complex than the pedagogical demands of monoculturalism.

10. Last, demographic trends tell us that we must prepare the next generation of teachers to meet these demands.

CONCLUSION

What, then, have we learned in school?

Unquestionably, teaching and learning about these issues is difficult, at times painful, usually ragged and lacking closure—just as there are no easy solutions to the issues that courses such as this explore.

But what our students can gain in such courses is a greater understanding of themselves and each other, and the factors that unite and divide us. They learn something of what hurts and what helps each other and why, and this can be the beginning of more informed and conscious thought, growth, and action. As educators, to be part of this process is deeply rewarding.

Most compelling of the lessons, though, is that many of our students hunger for the kind of understanding courses such as this can provide. They hunger to understand what they already see and feel. They come to us brimming with questions, wanting to have their perceptions of their world acknowledged, clarified, challenged, or explained. If ever there were golden moments for education, they are these. As educators we are privy every day to seeing our students seize on and use what we and their classmates can provide for them out of our collective knowledge of materials, resources, and issues. This particular course is always oversubscribed, and the effects of the course linger long after the course is over. As one returning student said months after the course had ended, "It opened up a whole new world."

Given the national climate of cultural distrust and tensions, can we afford not to respond to these students' needs to understand their world? Can we afford not to continue to try, against all challenges, to address directly these pressing issues? The class on Issues of Race and Culture offers us one glimpse of how that might be done.

CHAPTER 5

IDEALIZATION, DISILLUSIONMENT, AND REPARATION IN TEACHING ABOUT RACE AND CULTURE

The solid, bright blue video screen yields to the image of a classroom at the University of Pennsylvania. A professor of law paces in front of 105 students in one of the nation's most prestigious universities and poses a question that goes unanswered. Searching for a way to animate his somnolent students, Professor Murray Dolfman says, "We have some ex-slaves here. They should know [the 13th Amendment] by heart." He turns to a young Black man. "Would you read it for us, please?" He compliments the young man on a reading job well done. Then he adds, "As a former slave myself, I hold that Amendment very close to my heart. We Jews were once held in bondage by pharaohs, so every year we celebrate our liberation at Passover." And shortly the class ends.

But within several days, a contingent of Black students visits Professor Dolfman at his office and explains they were deeply offended by his use of the term "ex-slaves" and by his singling out the young Black man in that context. He apologizes, but they contend that the apology is insufficient. Over the next several months, amid heightened tensions on campus, Professor Dolfman is "sentenced," in the words of a White history professor, to "thought reform" with a social worker and suspended for two semesters. The next year he is allowed to resume teaching evening classes. The professor of history likens the handling of the episode to tactics in Beijing. Professor Houston Baker, Jr., the Black director of the university's Center for the Study of Black Literature and Culture, says the campus will be a better place for the incident. And for the viewers, the filmmaker moves on to another story of "campus culture wars" (Pack & Prizer, 1993).

The lights flicker on in our classroom filled with 25 high school juniors and seniors who have elected to take a course called "Issues of Race and Culture." Over the next hour these students, roughly 25 percent of whom are students of color, will wrestle with issues suggested by the video. By the end of class there will be anger, tears, a hushed embarrassment, and confusion. What begins as a tentative exploration of what they perceive as a professor's insensitivity or students' hypersensitivity becomes a heated and emotional conversation which reveals the difficulties in working with these issues.

Vital and involved, these young thinkers have elected this course because they are interested in learning more about issues of race and culture. For the next five months, they will explore lives and issues of Native Americans, African Americans, Jewish Americans, Asian Americans, and Latinos. Because the course is team-taught and interdisciplinary, they will do so through the lenses of historians, cultural anthropologists, filmmakers, novelists, and poets from multiple cultures. But their journeys of discovery will also, most likely, take them from idealization through disillusionment, and, if we and they are lucky, into a reparation which strengthens their sense of self and commitment to the larger world. They will come to know, as one author has suggested about the process of living with these issues, "It isn't easy. It never has been easy" (Silko, 1977).

THE APPEAL OF THE IDEAL

With the difficulties inherent in discussions of race and culture, why do these adolescents and we teachers who work with them take ourselves into the arena of such a class?

Since the course is elected, each student is there by choice. Each has decided for different reasons that he or she is willing to endure the reported tensions and awkwardness that surround discussions in the course, as well as the repeated challenges to his or her views and sense of self that are a natural part of reading and talking about these issues from multiple viewpoints.

What all of these students share is a hunger to understand more about issues that surround them every day—in school or beyond. They want to know more about racism and prejudice and stereotypes. They want to know more about separatism, integration, and assimilation. They want to know more about history and cultures—their own and each other's. And they want to know more about public policy.

As one student wrote on the first day of class, "I'm curious about the tension between African Americans and Jews. Often the cultures have been compared to each other, yet more and more the tension builds. Where did it begin and how can it be solved?"

Or another: "I'm troubled by the anger that minorities turn on White strangers. I don't know how to respond to that."

Or: "Should different ethnic groups that come to this country become part of it, learn the language and the customs, and become Americans? Or should groups strive to maintain their culture and language, which then ends up segregating them from others? Should we live in diverse neighborhoods as Americans, or in segregated neighborhoods based on culture?"

Some come into the course sharing Malcolm X's view that "democracy is hypocrisy." Their personal histories have already steeped them in disillusionment about many aspects of race or culture, but they want to discuss the issues, one student admitting she had "been waiting four years to talk about these things." Others, frustrated by painful moments in their own lives, come seeking solutions to the racial or cultural problems that color their world. Still others, to varying degrees, believe that they themselves are free from the racism and biases that characterize many of those around them, and as Andrew Hacker (1995) would suggest of such young liberals, pride themselves on this type of involvement with the issues. All of these students believe that studying the issues and learning more about each other will matter. They hold dear the ideal of a school that is free from the prejudices beyond its doors and a nation that can move closer to living out its own ideals. They want to know what can be done to make things better, and they want to be part of that process. They are curious, committed, and willing to take risks. At times, they are also exceedingly vulnerable.

A related set of ideals binds the two of us who teach these adolescents. With backgrounds in history and literature, respectively, and long committed to issues of social justice, we have come ourselves from divided childhood societies in the South and West of the 1950s. We learned young—as these students have—the destructiveness of cultural tensions and the frustration of being unable to understand better those tensions. We saw, as these students do, how much those divisions hurt those around us. We believe that education can and does make a difference in the nature of a life and in the nature of a community, and that there is a fundamental difference for these students between learning from books and learning from each other's lives. We believe that it is important to expose the students to numbers of significant thinkers on the issues, to help them understand how to assess situations from multiple individual and cultural perspectives, and to give them experience in doing so.

We also believe that it is important to help students name and discuss their confusions, and to verify or challenge their assumptions—that is, to help them move closer to understanding their world. We know we are teachers and not facilitators or therapists, and we are there, as Paulo Freire has said, to teach. But we also know we need, at times, the wisdom not only of the teacher, but of the facilitator and the therapist as well.

THE INEVITABLE DISILLUSIONMENT

Perhaps because ideals and hopefulness figure largely in the mindsets of us all, as we wrestle with the issues, disillusionment is inevitable and is tied to an iconoclasm unavoidable in discussing these issues from perspectives grounded in multiple cultures.

The readings, films, speakers, and discussions bring forward ideas that constantly challenge these students' current perceptions. The materials and the process of examining them result in students thinking about their own and others' attitudes and behaviors. Sometimes the materials illuminate moments, trigger memories, stir stories. Sometimes they lead to profound personal discoveries revealed spontaneously, viscerally, in the public glare of a group discussion or recorded in the privacy of journals or papers. The students struggle with: "Who am I?" "Who are you?" and "Who are we?" And during their months together, these students will most likely have moments when they experience, articulate, or quietly reveal disillusionment associated with themselves, each other, their families, whole cultures, or their nation as they struggle to come to terms with the discrepancy between their ideals and the realities being brought before them by scholars, artists, teachers, and classmates. They may also become disillusioned with the course itself, the teachers, or the process of studying and talking with each other about the issues. Nor are those of us who work with these students immune to disillusionment.

In the discussion centering on the law class at the University of Pennsylvania, what has begun as a rather safe analysis of Professor Dolfman's controversial circumstances soon becomes a profoundly personal and emotional exchange.

In this discussion, one student, whose family roots lay in Russia, has been experiencing a powerful sense of her cultural identity and has felt a need to explore, clarify, and protect that aspect of herself. She has also felt criticized by others when she has spoken out on issues. She speaks bluntly and passionately to the class, explaining that such criticism can make communication about these issues impossible.

Another student explains this is why some students choose not to take the course. "They feel they'd have to censor themselves as a result of being accused of being a racist. They are afraid of accusations."

At this point, a young Middle Eastern woman, attached to the school and comfortable with her own relationship to the issues and to others in the group, recalls a racial incident in the school several years before. Troubled both by this memory of discord and by the growing tension in the present discussion, she whispers, "The hate . . . " and breaks down.

I too am shaken. As this earnest young woman collapses in tears, I feel a familiar paralysis, knowing I am in charge. I am an adult who must make a split-second decision, in front of a group, about where to take this moment. I am aware of infinite levels of concern: for this child; for the students who stare or avert their eyes in discomfort; for the complexity of the moment; for the difficulties, once again, of doing this kind of course. As the moment and the class draw to a close, my colleague and I offer a few clarifying and supportive words to the group, and the class ends.

What is the net effect of such moments for these students? Will the moment forever be encased in emotional discomfort that will be carried forward into future engagements with the issues? Will the moment alter in some subtle or profound way for better or worse their image or understanding of themselves or each other? Most likely I will never know.

I am personally averse to anything resembling "sensitivity games," and a part of me recoils at the thought that the classroom has become something other than the arena of safe, intellectual discussions. But I am gently reminded by my partner that whenever there is discussion of issues involving race, and power, and identity, we leave the zones of safe talk behind. "It's not bad," he says, "for students to learn that what they say offends others." In the safety of our partnership, I know I too will be able to take the next steps next week. But I am also reminded how difficult it would be to travel this pedagogical journey alone.

Other equally potent moments come to mind. Experience teaches us that in this kind of course, students will experience many moments that can be iconoclastic in nature.

Sometimes disillusionment for these students is centered around something no less fundamental than their sense of self. Hearing the way their classmates, especially those from other cultures, view particular attitudes or decisions can result in students regularly calling into question their own choices and behaviors. But the self-doubt may cut deeper.

Some students are thrust into what is for them disturbing reflections on the nature of their own racial or cultural identity. Although such moments may be related to the natural process and stages of constructing a racial identity (Tatum, 1992), they can still be troubling. For some students, readings in the course stir memories of attempting to come to terms with disillusionment over their sense of self as very young children. For one child, safety from judgment based on skin color, even at home, could be found only in constructing a special place to play, alone. For others, disparaging messages about their identity arrived in the voices of playmates—at the back door, in the neighborhood, or in special activities.

Because this course focuses primarily on issues emerging from several cultures of color, some White students feel that representation of their lives has been left out. Although there may be many moments in texts and in discussions when their culture has been implicated in acts of prejudice or racism, they may feel they have been unable to identify with central situations discussed in the course or to understand the concept of culture as it relates to their own White identity. For some White students, the accumulation of such moments results in their feeling that they have "no culture at all." Additionally, it is often particularly thoughtful and sensitive students who elect to take the course. They enter the course already tending toward introspection. As course discussions center not only on cultural richness, but also on acts of injustice, especially on the part

of the dominant White culture, White students may internalize these discussions
and find the burden of guilt, confusion, or self-doubt insupportable. For some,
it means going through periods when they want to reject their Whiteness or their
own culture. Or they struggle to find ways to integrate what may be distinctly
negative aspects of their own cultural or national history with previous images
that they have nurtured and that are now being challenged by these additional
points of view. The intensity of their emotions may also result in a heightened
frustration with their classmates, with us, with the authors or artists who bring
unwanted messages, or with the process of examining the issues. For several
students, questions and frustrations about being White have resulted in an intentional sustained withdrawal from class discussions—as one student phrased it,
a prolonged "angry silence."

For some students disillusionment surrounds not self, but family. Students
may struggle with being torn between what they are hearing or learning about
in class and what they know of their family's attitudes or choices. Exploration
of historical acts of oppression in the course can result in students examining in
a new light the lives and choices of parents or grandparents or long-standing
family friends. In such moments students are forced into a type of solitary exploration of conflicting views involving individuals close to them. How do they
reconcile what scholars or artists or classmates are saying and their closeness to
family friends, relatives, or members of their own family? For one young man,
the thrust of class discussions triggered an inward journey into the past of his
family in Europe and the United States and the role that key relatives played in
government decision making. For this student, the naturally emerging ideas of
his classmates in a single series of discussions challenged directly the images
of his relatives handed down in family lore. Aside from sharing his frustrations
with us, it would be he alone who would have to come to terms with the ensuing
inner conflict.

Even the act of noting similarities across cultures can lead students to articulate these moments of deep-seated personal disillusionment. In one assignment,
students are asked to describe a similarity between an aspect of life described
in a Latino novel and an aspect of life in their own culture. For one young man,
Sandra Cisneros's lyrical novel about a Latino neighborhood, *The House on
Mango Street* (1989), called forward disillusioning realizations about the meaning of home. His parents' divorce had meant for this child weekday and weekend homes, but little sense of belonging. In another paper, a student took the
reader on a guided tour of her lavishly appointed apartment. As she looked out
over the empty rooms, she agreed with Cisneros, that "a house does not make
a home."

The complex, intractable nature of the issues or the multiple points of view
put forward in discussions may also cause or deepen students' feelings of disillusionment with classmates. Students' dramatically diverging viewpoints on sig-

nificant issues or their inability to understand or be sensitive to each other's points of view may suddenly or gradually disillusion them about even trying to engage in studying the issues. Students who say, "You can never understand what it's like," referring to their own racial or cultural experiences, frustrate those who are making a determined effort to understand other lives. Students also know they are expending a great deal of intellectual and emotional effort to work with the issues and with each other, and yet they may see the tensions among them persist or even mount—in class, in hallways, in assemblies. Then they wonder: Why isn't what we are doing here making things better? And if this process won't make things better, then what is the point of trying?

During one discussion, I look at a young Black woman across the room. This smart, politically astute, passionate, articulate young woman is withdrawing gradually from the group. Despite the support my teaching partner and I can offer her as discussions unfold or through ongoing dialogues with her, eventually she will cease to fight at all for her point of view. She knows that not one of her classmates shares her perspective. And I know I cannot ever really know or fight her battles. I cannot alter the nature of the experiences she has shared with us. At times her isolation overwhelms me with sorrow—for her, for all of us. I cannot take back words said or images revealed in the flow of these discussions. A sense of personal failure and limitation threatens to engulf me. I cannot save even one of these children, open-eyed to the world, from harm.

Sometimes, even the group as a whole is rendered silent. In the wake of a video on gangs in South Central Los Angeles, the room is quiet. Gradually, students make observations about the lure of gangs as suggested by those interviewed—the need for power, for a family, for protection, for a future. Near the end of class, one student who has felt the effects of gang life close to home speaks up. He is trembling. "I hear everyone speaking. It's so unreal. I know if I speak it will seem like 'Black rage.' I have so much grief, so much grief in me." None of the other students know how to respond.

There are also moments when disillusionment centers on the course itself, the materials, the pedagogy, or us teachers who bear responsibility for shaping the course. Points of view that challenge directly the students' own points of view or those of their families can cause students to strike out at an author, a message, an approach, or us. And at some point, these students, in all their earnestness and commitment to addressing the issues, will come to understand not only the degree to which the problems have eluded solutions, but the limitations of talk and study as well—that is, the limitation of the very process in which they are engaged.

In particularly potent discussions of a little booklet called "Cultural Etiquette: A Guide for the Well Intentioned" (Three Rivers, 1991), White students, deeply resentful of the author's confrontational approach, have attacked the credibility of the author, defiled her name, or walked out and slammed the door. In other instances, students' increasing frustration over their classmates' lingering inability to share their concerns—whether over the fragmenting of the nation into individual cultures or on affirmative action—have led them to such anger that they say it has damaged their outlook on the course. In one discussion, the bitterly harsh statistics used by Andrew Hacker to describe Black life in America (1995) caused several students to call into question the focus and process of the class altogether, suggesting with great emotion that all such information does is to reinforce negative thinking about Blacks. In another moment, Hacker's description of liberals (1995) resulted in several students raised in distinctly liberal households rejecting much of his position altogether, with one student suggesting that if this was the kind of reading we would be doing in the course, she would drop it. And sometimes, as in the discussion about the incident at the University of Pennsylvania, individual frustration and disillusionment can result in tears. How do students feel, now or in the future, about such moments?

Thus, even with our having laid ground rules for discussing the issues, the room inevitably, at times, is a place of tension. The group divides. Someone becomes teary or enraged, slams a door—or withdraws into silence and isolation.

Partly because of these moments we witness among our students, we teachers, too, experience doubt and disillusionment. Knowing that we are responsible for this forum means we reexamine all of our choices. Have we made the most responsible choices in selecting the materials and the pedagogy? As discussion moderators, have we intervened soon enough in volatile discussions? Have we made the most sound and useful decisions in key moments as discussions have unfolded and students have openly challenged or confronted each other? Have we responded in a thoughtful and timely enough manner when students have come to us—alone or in groups—about frustration they can no longer manage on their own? Are our students developmentally ready—even at 16, 17, or 18—to engage in discussions that trigger such anger, sadness, or frustration? And if not now, when?

At the other extreme, we constantly ask ourselves: Has the course done what it could do? Has it broadened these students' thinking? Has it helped them begin to develop a more polycultural perspective as they assess moments and situations around them or as they engage in daily decision making in their own lives? Have we been able to offer them an opportunity for growth that will matter? Or is the experience mostly one of disorientation or loss? Are there so many potent factors involved in these issues that discussing them is, as some have recently suggested, ultimately useless—just more talk? Although on one hand both of us agree that education must take on the challenges of educating the next generation of students to function more successfully in a multicultural society, the intensity and the difficulties of this kind of teaching produce a host of uncertainties for us as teachers.

CULTIVATING REPARATION

What are the short- and long-term effects of these moments of ideological colli-sion or bone-cutting personal realizations triggered by examining, in a class, issues of race and culture? When disillusionment has torn at the edges of our idealism, how do we move forward toward growth?

Without meaning to overdramatize, I sometimes find myself feeling echoes of Samuel Beckett: "I cannot go on." But I also recall the wishes of Shelby Steele, who calls for the continued effort needed to converse about race (1993). And this is what we do. We make the effort. We continue to gather three times a week to examine materials and issues and to talk with each other. And, without fail, many of the wounds begin to crust over.

Most interestingly, even in the toughest moments, it is the students them-selves who begin, immediately, the reparative process. Some seek us out to talk or leave us a note. Some make choices that enable them to take their own steps forward. They talk with friends or their family or they write about their frustra-tions in journal entries. Useful in many respects, the course journals allow stu-dents to engage in a centuries-old gesture—using writing to give order and meaning to the essential disorder of life. The journals also allow students to conduct private dialogues with us as we respond to their entries. Some students speak in class of their disillusionment and call on classmates or on us to use class time to help them understand what they are experiencing. And some, rec-ognizing the raw need in front of them, reach out to their classmates long before they are asked.

During such moments I am repeatedly struck by the depth as well as the vulnerability of these students. And I know I must try to support them in ways that I am not sure I even know.

For the students who have been so upset by our use of Hacker's *Two Na-tions* (1995), we meet with them and explain some of the difficulties in choosing and working with materials in this kind of course. We try to use acknowledged spokespersons in the field, we explain, and to use ways of working with texts that will help students understand what the authors are saying. But we do not necessarily know ahead of time how the texts will affect students or discussions, and it may not be clear, in the fast pace of a class discussion, exactly the best moment to intervene. As we leave these students, I am reminded that I cannot control or undo the individual ways in which students may experience a particu-lar class. And I do not know what those classroom moments will mean for them, in the short term or the long term.

For the students who have questioned their Whiteness in their own dark nights of the soul, we remind them about our study of racial identity develop-ment models (Tatum, 1992) and that many Whites—of any age—may experi-ence these feelings as part of the natural process of developing a racial identity. We reassure them that they are not alone and that as fine young thinkers and writers, they will be able to draw on their own significant strengths to deal with both their emotions and the issues. We suggest that the intentional withdrawal from class discussions is essentially one healthy way of allowing themselves time to integrate so much new and potent information. As some psychiatrists point out, learning involves an inner reorganization as we seek to accommodate new material (Fuqua, 1994, p. 81). We suggest that they give themselves time, trust themselves that they *will* find their own best way to live with and respond to these issues.

In thinking of several other students whose frustrations have been particularly poignant, I design a presentation for the school community around issues the students have so eloquently raised during the course. Drawing on their actual conversations and writings, I try to let them know that the questions they raise are worthy of a broad and thoughtful audience.

At times, the reparative process is best served by our moving on in the course, introducing additional viewpoints that help students place earlier points of view in a different perspective. The process may also mean establishing a kind of meta-perspective to help them understand why a particular point of view may be so difficult for them. It may mean reminding the students about the author's background or credentials, or reminding them, once again, that there is a wide range of diverging views on each of the issues. It is they who must ultimately weigh the value and the implications of each view. In the wake of the students' distress over the description of situations facing Black Americans in *Two Nations* (1995), we place Hacker's voice in perspective by listing on the board the 14 or so other points of view represented in our examination of African-American lives and issues.

Sometimes students are helped by our being open with them in class about our own doubts and uncertainties—the challenges involved in choosing texts and approaches and the unpredictability of the flow of discussions or the responses of students to familiar or unfamiliar material. And sometimes it helps to explain to them the cycle of emotions that may well accompany the study of these issues. We also underscore the need for long-term commitment, patience, and perseverance in addressing such difficult issues.

At all times, the reparative process means our supporting these students in ways that will encourage them to remain actively engaged with the issues. It means providing support for individual students and creating a reliable environment for the group. This is a process we have entered into together. We will not leave them. We know it is hard. We will see it through together, if they are willing.

And for our own disillusionment . . . for the days during which we say, "It's just too hard"? For us, team teaching has been invaluable. Ongoing collaboration allows us to share our concerns and seek solutions together. Then, we too move on. And always, for us there are the 25 new faces each year who come before us, questions in hand.

In the discussion involving the incident at the University of Pennsylvania, even as the group is dividing and breaking down, the students begin to offer several constructive ways of regarding what has unfolded. One underscores the virtue of being open with such concerns. Another suggests that in such a course, it would help to establish guidelines for discussions at the outset—something crucial we have always done in the course and did not do this year. Another suggests working on the problems as a school and not allowing them to be ignored. Yet another describes in his own way the usefulness of personal restraint:

> I wanted to do this course because all my life I've said things without thinking, rushed into things. But growing up, you can take a step back. You can say what you think, but you have the ability to restrain yourself as well. There's a limit to what you can say, and you have to find it for yourself. The older we get the more we find the limit. People can learn to look back and say, "That was wrong."

And at the end, after several moments of silence, a young Latina crosses the room and puts her arms around the young Middle Eastern woman who has cried. The reparative process involves both the mind and the heart.

Our own words, at the end of class, remind these students that adults experience similar challenges in talking about these issues, and in fact, often avoid doing so. Anyone reasonably sensitive to the issues has felt as they feel today. Learning how to talk with each other is a step in itself. We will all be here again next week, and we will go on, together.

During the next class, we move from the University of Pennsylvania to a small Black community in Ohio as we examine *Sula* (1973), a novel by Nobel Prize–winning author Toni Morrison. At the end of the class I have them read aloud the opening and closing paragraphs from Steele's essay on cross-racial conversations. What he describes is a congenial, integrated party on a warm summer evening in California. The relaxed mood of a conversation is broken when a Black engineer raises the issue of race as it involves his daughter attending a predominantly White private school. The host and hostess, uncomfortable, intervene by offering drinks, at which point these adults, professionals and intellectuals all, retreat into their safe and separate worlds. Steele recalls his disappointment: "No matter how badly it might have gone for us that warm summer night, we should have talked. We should have made the effort" (1993, p. 228).

Steele's words reassure us that in these matters, conversation is a form of taking action. The ability to talk with each other, in and of itself, is a significant act. They have been willing, already, I tell these students, to move further than many adults.

As we reflect on our own emotional discussion, a White student explains, "On the news the other night, Rodney King said, 'Can't we all just get along?'

That's how I felt after our discussion. It happens again and again. We can't get along. I felt so pessimistic."

But across from him, the young Latina who has soothed her teary classmate says, "I think the class was very good and I hope we can have more like it. It opens eyes and we all become more open minded to see others' views as well as our own. Now we can start to get something done."

LOOKING BACK

Although we have not yet arrived at the end of this year's course, some of the words left behind by former students offer a glimpse of how some of these students may ultimately experience the ebb and flow of emotions involved in exploring these issues.

For some students, moments that created the most anguish as the course unfolded are seen in retrospect as the most illuminating. They become "defining moments." As one young Latina later explained about the painful class on Hacker's statistics on Black Americans (1995), "I felt I had learned an important lesson—the dangers of generalization. I know this might have been a somewhat defining moment for you, as teachers of this course, too. I think you both saw the importance of making clear that this is only one perspective. . . . " And about one of the teaching moments that created the most doubt for me, a student remarked, "It was really helpful. It made us think about so many things—about how even unintentionally we can violate someone's feelings."

From a young White student who had stressed, throughout the course, the need for a multicultural perspective:

> I like the way [historian] Ronald Takaki used the idea of a different mirror. I keep on coming back to that because it seems essential to my understanding or empathy with [people from] other races. To be a true humanitarian in the world today, it takes an ability to empathize with others and to try to look through that different mirror. It made me happy when I could look around the classroom and see and hear people doing that essential thinking.

And from one particularly introspective young woman who identified herself as "part White, part Asian":

> To me, this class doesn't really end here. It's more of a beginning. I must say that it definitely has me thinking about identity. How do I define myself? How do others define themselves, and what experiences lead them to think of themselves that way? The answers aren't always definite, but the fact

that someone can ask these questions and at least try to hear and understand what the next person has to say is a good start.

As for myself, I still look back on the anger and tears and wonder what it means. Have some students gained insight at the expense of others? Is in fact this kind of learning too rough sometimes on these budding selves? And of course, will these explorations eventually make any difference at all in these students' lives or in the lives of those around them?

But I also remember a moment, months after the course has ended one year. In a nearly deserted hallway after school, a heated argument has erupted among several students planning a celebration for Martin Luther King Day. The young Black student who shared his grief over neighborhood gangs steps into the argument, and with his words, begins to quell the tension and enable the students to discuss their differences. "What we have here," he says, "are two issues of race and culture."

I think back over the course with its countless ragged edges, the hopefulness at its core, as well as its moments of fear and trembling.

Maybe it's not such a bad start, after all.

CONCLUSION

Beneath these students' academic or emotional interest in these issues is often a yearning for specific answers to the problems that surround them, a yearning to have their own perspectives and values confirmed, and a yearning to be reassured that an involvement with the issues can and will make a difference. In reality, they will discover that there are no single answers to the problems associated with the issues and that they must decide for themselves the most effective approach for addressing them. They will realize that the effects of their study will be limited. And they may find themselves less—not more—secure in their own positions. But they will leave the course with a broader understanding of significant issues, each other, and themselves. Some will feel less fear of talking with others about such issues. And all of the students recognize that they have engaged themselves seriously and thoughtfully with key issues of our times.

Courses like this are built on a respect for honest dialogue and critical thinking, and a focus on real events. They loosen the walls among school, home, and community. They make clear that such study is open-ended, and that coming to terms with the frustrations aroused in the process will not end with the last day of class.

As adults associated with such study, we must ask ourselves what legacy we as a nation have left these students: when children seek the safety of a hideout to assure themselves of the worth of their own skin; when gangs define the perimeter of a home; or when the lingering effects of history still tear us apart. What does it mean when all of these students wonder, along with a tele-vised Rodney King, "Can't we all just get along?"

We must acknowledge that studying these issues will result in repeated challenges to the youthful idealism that brings students into such a course. But we also might remember the words of Robert Coles as he studied such idealism in the South of the 1960s: "Idealism can generate moments of despair, but some-times there is a subsequent burst of energy and enthusiasm—the consequence of realizing that generosity has its restorative possibilities as well as its frustra-tions" (1986, p. 193). Or the words of one of those "youthful idealists" he interviewed: "[It's] good: to lose one's illusions! It is dangerous to walk the earth among others, and not see oneself through their eyes" (Coles, 1986, p. 194).

Courses such as the one described here are important because they represent a form of study we must engage in. Knowing more about these issues and about how to understand and live with each other directly affects the quality of our lives as individuals and as a nation. It is also a form of study that is complex, difficult, awkward, painful, and in many ways unfamiliar. We simply do not do it very often. But it is being cast as "dumb" by antimulticulturalists who under-stand neither the compelling need for such study nor the ongoing difficulty of engaging in it. Nor do they understand its often profound effects. We must come to understand and appreciate the full range of psychological and social chal-lenges inherent in these students' needs to know more about these issues and in the process of study itself. And we must know how better to address them. Not to take up this challenge and not to avail ourselves of the resources to make it possible is to cut ourselves off from one of the great learning opportunities before us for the twenty-first century.

CHAPTER 6

WHY I AM A MULTICULTURALIST

The Power of Stories Told and Untold

In the climactic scene of Toni Morrison's novel *Beloved* (1987), we watch in horror as an escaped slave named Sethe rounds up her four children, takes them into an empty woodshed, and begins to slaughter them. Seeing her former owner approaching, Sethe has opted to kill her own children rather than see them grow up in slavery. Coming not solely from the reaches of the writer's imagination, Sethe's story is modeled on the life of an actual slave named Margaret Garner, who, in the ultimate act of love, had decided that under slavery, her children were safer dead.

Morrison tells us she has given us Sethe's story to help us rediscover our "disremembered" past, a history of America we have chosen to forget (Benson, 1987). Such is only one power of works like *Beloved*.

As someone who teaches a course on issues of race and culture to high school students, I know that reading and listening to each other's stories across racial and cultural lines, far from serving to disunite us, as some would have us believe, give us tools for survival in this multicultural nation. Works by such writers as Morrison, Leslie Marmon Silko, James Baldwin, Maxine Hong Kingston, Bernard Malamud, and Sandra Cisneros, and the conversations they evoke, engage us in thinking about our own and each other's lives in real and significant ways. I know beyond doubt, beyond pages and pages of theory and acrimonious debate over multiculturalism, that these works open up, clarify, affirm, and support lives and possibilities.

KNOWING OURSELVES AND OTHERS

My interest in these works comes from working with students as an English teacher in public and private high schools in New York City, Boston, Los Angeles, and Chicago. But my relationship with the works was born in a child-hood divided between the Jim Crow South and the urban North. From the North I gained an outside perspective on the South and the knowledge that there existed a social structure other than one founded on segregation. The South forged in me a lifelong need for these texts.

In a recent review of the short stories of William Trevor, Reynolds Price remarks that the great voices of fiction writing and perhaps the writers' reasons for writing are often "grounded in a single scene . . . the physical moment in which a single enormous question rose before a watchful child and fueled the lifelong search for an answer" (1993, p. 1). Perhaps the same can be said for avid readers.

The segregated South of the 1940s and 1950s had the curious effect of creating a simultaneous intimacy and unbridgeable distance between many Blacks and Whites. For me, as a White child, this combination resulted in a pressing need to understand at an early age issues of race and culture, issues which, for reasons of the social situation itself, could not be explained by either the Whites or the Blacks around me. Whites were too committed to maintaining the status quo, and Blacks had too much to lose to risk being honest about race to a White child. As Lillian Smith has written in her eloquent essays of that time and place, "the southern child adjusted himself to his world in which people said what they did not mean, and meant what they dared not say" (1949, p. 109).

Unable to find the clarity I needed from those around me, I turned to books to supply the answers. Whatever editing or censorship Black writers might face once the manuscripts left their hands, the writing began as a private act, apart from the power and scrutiny of Whites, and thus, I reasoned, an honest one. Richard Wright, James Baldwin, and Jean Toomer could tell me what neither Whites nor Blacks I had grown up with would tell me. They could tell me a truth about my life. Later, when I began teaching in urban settings, I knew that if these stories had helped me live my life, they had that same potential for my students. That belief has been more than borne out over the years, whether in a public school in East Harlem in the 1970s or a private progressive school in Chicago in the 1990s.

Like *Beloved*, some of these works bring forward lost or unknown histories. For many students today, a working familiarity with their own cultural history and the wish for that history to be known by others are essential steps in the formation of their identities. Such knowledge is not always easy to come by. For example, as Morrison has remarked, for years we have engaged in a type of national amnesia about slavery. It was "not a story to pass on." It is the duty, she says, of artists now to tell that story, to make sure it is known (Benson, 1987). A few days after reading *Beloved*, one student whose own family history had been shaped by acts of racial violence said of the novel, "It was so big sometimes I couldn't even hold it. Everything that happened to my ancestors was there. She said it to the class so I didn't have to." In the mind of this student, Morrison had succeeded in giving her back her past.

Others of these works help us comprehend and shape our lives as they unfold. As one student said after reading Gloria Naylor's *The Women of Brewster Place* (1982), "I carry it around with me. I live on the South Side, and every block has a little Brewster Place in it." Or the student who wrote of Sandra Cisneros's *The House on Mango Street* (1989): "Although Esperanza is still a small child, she can see the racial barriers between neighborhoods, and the colors that separate her from others. This rings true in Chicago today. On many occasions people refer to Cabrini Green as a war zone. But those people forget that Cabrini Green is someone's neighborhood. That neighborhood holds someone's house, husband, wife, and children." Through Cisneros's gentle and poetic tutelage, we come to know that all neighborhoods, even ones we are quick to call "bad," are someone's home and that how we speak of them matters. These works can sustain us, and through them we can try to live a more conscious life.

They also help us in knowing each other. Forty years after *Brown v. Board of Education*, in this heterogeneous society, the overwhelming majority of us still live largely segregated lives. This is especially significant for our students, who, as the next generation to oversee and shape the nation's institutions, are gaining little experience in relating to one another across racial or cultural lines. Studies by Harvard University have found "schools resegregating at the fastest rate since the 1954 *Brown v. Board of Education* ruling" (Applebome, 1997, p. A8), and school integration "nonexistent" in America's big cities (Grossman, Kirby, Leroux, & Thomas, 1994, p. 12). Ultimately, this harms us all, as living apart we come to know little of each other or each other's needs or joys. The works of these writers, however, begin to lower the barriers between us. As one student said of a James Baldwin story of a lynching (1965), "I didn't know that had happened. I needed to know that." Or the student who said of a small pamphlet on cultural etiquette by Native-American writer Amoja Three Rivers (1991), "It was hard to read. We saw things we didn't want to see. We saw we had done things that hurt others, and we didn't know it hurt."

The distances that divide us are rendered more salient by the fact that they are rarely bridged by meaningful conversations. Because conversations with each other about each other across cultural lines can be awkward, embarrassing, or painful, rarely do we engage in them. But the works of these writers invite us to do so. They invite us into unfamiliar lives and neighborhoods and communities, and they give us a common focus for dialogues. They help us talk about aspects of our lives that are difficult to discuss and about pressing issues that affect us all. In the process, drawing on our individual wisdoms, we share authority. However temporarily, we create a democracy of shared power. We learn about anti-Semitism from the student who says, "The first time I went into my backyard, the neighbor said, 'You dirty Jew.'" We learn about racism from the student who says, "I didn't know I was Black until the bus driver said to my mother, 'Not you, you Black bitch.'"

As a teacher, I believe these conversations matter—not only now, but in the future, as these students take positions of influence in society. I have to believe that what they have heard each other say will matter—will lead them toward humane ways of thinking and behaviors that can benefit us all. Without these works and the conversations they evoke, we can only imagine the lives and needs of each other. And so the works of these writers have helped me direct my own life and guide the lives of my students toward greater understanding, humility, and grace.

INCLUDING AND EXCLUDING LIVES

One reason these works are able to evoke such intense involvement on the part of students is the intimate connection students feel with the works' literary terrain. Although great works of literature transcend cultural boundaries, they are always rooted in the specifics of a culture, and those specifics often offer the reader a sense of familiarity which operates alongside universal aspects of the works. All students deserve knowing they can find that familiarity among the offerings in their courses. Paula Gunn Allen has described the impact of recently available Native-American literature on young Native-American readers: "Now we can say . . . I know these places, I know the landscape, I know the people, I know the sounds. I know, I understand. It's giving us our sanity back, person by person, and tribe by tribe" (Coltelli, 1990, p. 19).

For students of color, this familiarity also has more expansive consequences. A knowledge of these writers means knowing their literary history as well as the role models for a life with literature. In her autobiography, Gwendolyn Brooks laments she had not even heard of *The Souls of Black Folk* until she was grown (1972, p. 175). According to the editor of *Black Voices*, in the 1960s, Jonathan Kozol, then a teacher in an inner city public school in Boston, was fired for teaching the Langston Hughes poem "Ballad of the Landlord" to his class (Chapman, 1968, p. 425). Poet Sonia Sanchez remarked several years ago in an interview, "In high school and college American literature contained no black writers. As a consequence, the only time I saw 'me' was in sociology courses, and then I was an aberration. . . . That's really a terrible commentary on education" (Sanchez, 1983, p. 147). And recently, in the public schools of Chicago, one young teacher had to bring in his own materials to expose students to the work of writers of color (anonymous teacher, personal communication, fall 1990). Although these observations span several generations, they all suggest the same regret concerning inadequate coverage of the literature of writers of color in schools.

Some of today's most celebrated writers still struggle with the effects of a lack of exposure to their artistic roots and potential role models, based in curricular decisions of their schools. Both Alice Walker and Toni Morrison have spoken of the impact of the lack of role models. Writes Walker, "Mindful that throughout my four years at a prestigious black and then a prestigious white college I had heard not one word about early black women writers, one of my first tasks was simply to determine whether they had existed. After this, I could breathe easier, with more assurance about the profession I myself had chosen" (1983, p. 9).

Not to teach these works has broader implications as well. As Paul Lauter notes in the introduction to *Reconstructing American Literature*, "Our curricula have validated certain experiences at the expense of others. . . . The pictures they present to students of the American literary imagination or of American life and thought are woefully incomplete and inaccurate" (1983, pp. xv–xvi, xii). And as Paula Wehmiller has said, "When we don't know each other's stories, we will substitute our own myths, and probably hurt someone" (1991).

Further, to fully appreciate the impact of excluding these writers, members of the majority culture have to consider what it would mean to have our own cultural models excluded. What would be the impact, on ourselves and on our children, of courses excluding White writers? What would it mean to have White perspectives or cultural representatives and dynamics rarely, if ever, presented?

Ultimately, multicultural reading lists become models in themselves—not only as a more accurate reflection of the demographics of the culture, but as a model of inclusion based on merit.

The commitment to teach these works, however, is not broadly shared. Although they are considered some of the foremost writers in America today, they still do not have wide acceptance in the schools. As Henry Louis Gates points out—according to A. N. Applebee's "A Study of Book-Length Works Taught in High School English Courses" (1989)—today, even in schools with predominantly students of color, *all* of "the most frequently required" writers are White. "In public schools overall, only Lorraine Hansberry and Richard Wright appear among the top fifty authors required in English classes between grades 7 and 12." Moreover, Wright's *Black Boy* is among the books "most frequently banned from public schools." "Clearly," writes Gates, "the opening of the canon in traditional university literature departments has not yet affected the pedagogical practices of high school teachers" (1990, p. 13).

The effects of such practices reach well into the future. Recent articles have decried the decline in enrollment and completion of doctoral programs in the humanities by aspiring scholars of color. But should it be surprising that students of color would not be drawn into pursuing a field that has in many ways excluded them? The attraction of prospective scholars of color to the study of literature often begins with the discovery of their own literary world, through passionate seduction by their own literary history and the stunning successes of their greatest writers. It is the responsibility of the schools to provide this opportunity.

Therefore perhaps the question is not, "Why teach these works?" but rather, "What does it mean if we do *not* include these writers, since merit is beyond question?" This is the question that should haunt us.

A RESPONSE TO THE CRITICS

Despite the arguments for including the works of these writers, the broadening of course reading lists continues to arouse suspicion and discomfort in many quarters. Opposition to including these texts is widespread and vocal.

Some critics fear that including these works marks a politicization of the schools, a tainting of heretofore politically neutral environments. In her keynote address at the 1991 Chicago Humanities Festival, Toni Morrison addressed this argument by asking her audience to consider the realities of history. There are those, she suggested, who will have us believe in some "golden age" of education, some Edenic time of a nonpolitical academy. But, she posed, when *was* this time? As she moved deftly back through the decades, she made clear there was no golden age of the academy. Schools in each decade have, in fact, been surrounded by specific politically related factors which not only helped to mold them, but also made it impossible for them to live up to the ideals of education in a democratic society: the paucity of women and minorities in higher education at the turn of the century, the effects of the economic deprivation of the Depression, the constraints imposed by McCarthyism (Morrison, 1991).

Thus, schools have never existed completely apart from the political climates in which they function. Moreover, a democratization of reading lists marks a commitment not to a particular political ideology, but rather to an application of democratic principles and ideals within the school. Contrary to what many would have us believe today, through embracing the contributions of these writers, we have the opportunity to fashion a golden age of education, one in which we develop a democratic curriculum rooted in uncompromising artistic standards.

To do so, however, will mean, on the part of members of the majority culture—whether as teachers or students or writers—a sharing of power and centrality and prestige. And many are uncomfortable with that. Designing reading lists in which traditionally accepted writers share a focus with these equally talented writers may produce suspicion and criticism for less than noble reasons.

There is also the "zero-sum growth" argument: to include these writers is to exclude other—ostensibly "better," "greater"—writers. This argument overlooks at least three points.

First, in designing virtually any course, instructors must choose what to include and what to exclude. No matter the focus, not all "great," appropriate thinkers or artists can be included in a given course. There is simply not enough time to do so. So informed, discriminating choices always lie behind a syllabus. Always these choices result in some artists being included to the exclusion of others. Such is a reality of structuring a course. Always there are compelling thinkers excluded for lack of time.

Second, often, ironically, the very authors whom critics of multicultural reading lists cite to bolster exclusionary practices are the very thinkers who, as broad-minded humanists, would welcome new thinkers and writers into a center circle of shared thought. It would go against the central tenets of these great thinkers to exclude writers on the basis of race or culture or point of view, which, given the artistic merit of these works, one suspects, becomes the basis, at least in part, of their exclusion. After all, as Aristotle suggests in the *Metaphysics*, the pursuit of truth is best served by means of multiple paths: " . . . while individually we contribute little or nothing to the truth, by the union of all a considerable amount is amassed" (McKeon, 1941, p. 712).

Third, one must raise in this context the often recently debated question "Whose 'great books' are they?" Who, historically, has determined the nature of literary greatness, and what factors have underlain those determinations? Why, for example, in responding to criticism about the second edition of the famous Great Books series, did Mortimer Adler, editor of the series, declare there are no "Great Books" by Black writers before 1955? "This is the canon, and it's not revisable" (Blades, 1990, p. 14). The collection includes not one work by a Black-American writer. But again, it is Aristotle who reminds us that "best" remains at best a relative concept (McKeon, 1941, p. 1205). The varieties of powerful literary experiences and the moving testimonies of students whose lives have been shaped and turned by writers who speak to their worlds render such designations almost tangential—best for what? For whom?

Discomfort with these works emerges as well from their potential to affect and *move* students. As Paul Lauter has written, "As books speak out of social as well as private realities, so they speak to and help form us as social beings. They affect what we value, how we see, and perhaps even how we act" (1983, p. xxiv). The perspectives provided by these works help students appreciate:

1. The complexities of racial and cultural issues
2. The impact of our attitudes and behavior on each other across racial and cultural lines
3. The erroneous basis or dangers of narrowmindedness, however comforting it is at times
4. The impossibility of simple solutions to culturally based challenges.

Additionally, the structural and cultural complexities of works such as Silko's *Ceremony* (1977), Hinojosa's *This Migrant Earth* (1987), or Tan's *The Joy Luck Club* (1989) make it very difficult for students to continue to find tenable the assumptions that create stereotypes. The works become antidotes to stereotyping. Given the fact that by one estimate, by the year 2056, "whites may be a minority group" (Henry, 1990, p. 30), these are not insignificant considerations.

Further, for many of these writers there is an intimate link between their art and social action. As opposed to works that pose strictly philosophical questions, many of these works pose social questions, and responses to these questions on the part of students may include not only changes in the way the students think, but also an urge to act. The works often heighten students' awareness about our social failings as well as our social needs. To educate through these stories may be a call to action. Several graduates of the course I teach on issues of race and culture have returned to say they are choosing fields of work based on the explorations of the course.

Thus the way these works are regarded may reflect how we view the role of schools and education in society. To what degree are we willing, really, to educate students when the result of that education poses threats to the status quo? Poet Margaret Walker discovered one response to this question when the compiler of an anthology of ethnic literature for high school students was forbidden to include her major work "For My People" because it was "too militant" (Collier, 1984, p. 500).

Those in education who align themselves with Progressivism, however, have never shied away from linking education with social change. As George Counts wrote in the 1930s, "If the schools are to be really effective, they must become centers for the building, and not merely for the contemplation, of our civilization" (1969, p. 37).

For novelist Carlos Fuentes, these works help make that possible. In his 1994 address at the Art Institute of Chicago, Fuentes discussed several factors necessary to take us successfully into the twenty-first century. One was the ability to get along across cultures, and those he cited as helping us do that were Toni Morrison, Sandra Cisneros, Amy Tan, and Louise Erdrich—all writers, all women—all of whom envision through their art a world in which no one is excluded.

CONCLUSION

A few weeks ago, a student came into my office. She told me of a mother she knows whose only child, a son, 17, had just been killed by a gang member. In the wake of his death, the mother was peaceful, and had said of her son, "Now I know where he is at night. I know that he's safe."

What her story tells me is that more than 100 years after Margaret Garner took her four children into a woodshed in the "free" state of Ohio and began to kill them to keep them safe, some mothers in this country still feel that their children are safer dead.

That, it seems to me, is important for all of us to know.

In this era of deepening divisions among us, if we don't know and care about each other's stories, how can we possibly build together the nation we so boldly and radically dreamed some 200 years ago?

For all of these reasons, I am a multiculturalist. I believe in the power of the imagined stories of these writers and the real stories of my students as they discuss them, to change our lives for the better.

REFERENCES

Adams, M., Bell, L., & Griffin, P. (Eds.). (1997). *Teaching for diversity and social justice*. New York: Routledge.

Andersen, M., & Collins, P. H. (Eds.). (1995). *Race, class, and gender*. New York: Wadsworth.

Anson, R. S. (1987). *Best intentions: The education and killing of Edmund Perry*. New York: Random House.

Applebee, A. N. (1989). *A study of book-length works taught in high school English courses*, Report Series 1.2. Albany, NY: Center for the Learning and Teaching of Literature, University at Albany, State University of New York.

Applebome, P. (1995, March 1). Comparative literature: Times may change, but the writers students read stay much the same. *The New York Times*, p. B8.

Applebome, P. (1997, April 8). Schools see re-emergence of "separate but equal." *The New York Times*, p. A8.

Appleton, N. (1983). *Cultural pluralism in education: Theoretical foundations*. New York: Longman.

Arce, C. H. (1981). A reconsideration of Chicano culture and identity. *Daedalus, 110* (2), 177–191.

Aronson, E., & Thibodeau, R. (1992). The jigsaw classroom: A cooperative strategy for reducing prejudice. In J. Lynch, C. Modgil, & S. Modgil (Eds.), *Cultural diversity and the schools: Vol. II. Prejudice, polemic or progress?* (pp. 231–256). Bristol, PA: Falmer Press.

Baker, H. A., Jr. (1980). *The journey back: Issues in black literature and criticism*. Chicago: University of Chicago Press.

Baker, H. A., Jr. (Ed.). (1982). *Three American literatures*. New York: Modern Language Association of America.

Baker, H. A., Jr. (1987). *Modernism and the Harlem Renaissance*. Chicago: University of Chicago Press.

Baldwin, J. (1965). Going to meet the man. In J. Baldwin, *Going to meet the man* (pp. 198–218). New York: Dell.

Bambara, T. C. (1984). Salvation is the issue. In M. Evans (Ed.), *Black women writers 1950–1980: A critical evaluation* (pp. 41–47). New York: Anchor Books/Doubleday.

Banks, J. A. (1991, Spring). Multicultural literacy and curriculum reform. *Educational Horizons, 69*, 135–140.

Banks, J. A. (1993a). Approaches to multicultural curriculum reform. In J. A. Banks & C. A. McGee Banks (Eds.), *Multicultural education: Issues and perspectives* (pp. 195–214). Boston: Allyn & Bacon.

Banks, J. A. (1993b). The canon debate, knowledge construction, and multicultural education. *Educational Researcher, 22*(5), 4–14.

Banks, J. A., & Banks, C. A. McGee (Eds.). (1993). *Multicultural education: Issues and perspectives*. Boston: Allyn & Bacon.

Barnet, S. (1991, February 18). Get back. *The New Republic*, pp. 24–25.

Bell, D. (1992). *Faces at the bottom of the well: The permanence of racism*. New York: Basic Books.

Benson, A. (Director). (1987). *Toni Morrison*. [Video]. A London Weekend Television/RM Arts co-production from the series "Profile of a Writer." Public Media Home Vision.

Berman, P. (1994, February 28). The other and the almost the same. *The New Yorker*, pp. 61–71.

Bigsby, C. W. E. (1980). *The second black renaissance: Essays in black literature*. Westport, CT: Greenwood Press.

Blades, J. (1990, October 25). Expanded "great books" sure to open great debate. *Chicago Tribune*, Sec. 5, pp. 1, 14.

Bloom, A. (1987). *The closing of the American mind*. New York: Simon & Schuster.

Blos, P. (1941). *The adolescent personality*. New York: D. Appleton-Century.

Brooks, G. (1972). *Report from part one*. Detroit: Broadside Press.

Burbules, N. C., & Rice, S. (1991). Dialogue across differences: Continuing the conversation. *Harvard Educational Review, 61*, 393–416.

Caldwell, E., & Bourke-White, M. (1937). *You have seen their faces*. New York: Modern Age.

Carter, S. (1993). The black table, the empty seat, and the tie. In G. Early (Ed.), *Lure and loathing: Essays on race, identity, and the ambivalence of assimilation* (pp. 55–79). New York: Allen Lane/Penguin Press.

Chapman, A. (Ed.). (1968). *Black voices*. New York: New American Library.

Chin, F. (1991). *Donald duk*. Minneapolis: Coffee House Press.

Cisneros, S. (1989). *The house on Mango Street*. New York: Vintage.

Cochran, J. W. (1991). Halfbreed girl in the city school. In *Rethinking Columbus: A Special Edition of Rethinking Schools* (p. 48). Milwaukee: Rethinking Schools Ltd. in collaboration with the Network of Educators on Central America.

Coles, R. (1964). Children of crisis. A study of courage and fear. Boston: Little, Brown.

Coles, R. (1981). Minority dreams, American dreams. *Daedalus, 110*(2), 29–41.

Coles, R. (1986). *The moral life of children*. Boston: Houghton Mifflin.

Coles, R. (1993). *The call of service: A witness to idealism*. Boston: Houghton Mifflin.

Coles, R. (1995). *The story of Ruby Bridges*. New York: Scholastic.

Coles, R. (1997). *Doing documentary work*. New York: Oxford University Press.

Collier, E. (1984). Fields watered with blood: Myth and ritual in the poetry of Margaret Walker. In M. Evans (Ed.), *Black women writers 1950–1980: A critical evaluation* (pp. 499–510). New York: Anchor Books/Doubleday.

Coltelli, L. (1990). *Winged words: American Indian writers speak*. Lincoln, NE: University of Nebraska Press.

Cose, E. (1993). *The rage of a privileged class*. New York: HarperCollins.

Cotton, K. (1993, November). *Fostering intercultural harmony in schools: Research finding* [On line]. Topical Synthesis #7 in the School Improvement Research Series. (Downloaded 1997, April 8). http://www.nwrel.org/scpd/sirs/8/topsyn7.html

Counts, G. (1969). *Dare the school build a new social order?* New York: Arno Press and *The New York Times*.

Dewey, J. (1944). *Democracy and education*. New York: Free Press.

Dewey, J. (1963). *Experience and education*. New York: Collier Books/Macmillan.

Dewey, J., & Dewey, E. (1962). *Schools of tomorrow*. New York: E. P. Dutton.

Dilg, M. (1995). The opening of the American mind: Challenges in the cross-cultural teaching of literature. *English Journal, 84* (3), 18–25.

Dorfman, A. (1993, July). Afterword to *Death and the maiden*. Excerpted in *Stagebill*. Chicago: B & B Enterprises.

Dorris, M. A. (1981). The grass still grows, the rivers still flow: Contemporary Native Americans. *Daedalus, 110* (2), 43–69.

D'Souza, D. (1991). *Illiberal education: The politics of race and sex on campus*. New York: Free Press.

Dudley, W. (Ed.). (1991). *Racism in America: Opposing viewpoints*. San Diego, CA: Greenhaven Press.

Early, G. (1993). *Lure and loathing: Essays on race, identity, and the ambivalence of assimilation*. New York: Allen Lane/Penguin Press.

Edwards, R. G. (1993). Multiculturalism and its link to quality education and democracy. *MultiCultural Review, 2* (2), 12–14.

Erikson, E. H. (1963). *Childhood and society*. New York: W. W. Norton.

Erikson, E. H. (1980). *Identity and the life cycle*. New York: W. W. Norton.

"Ethnicity and education forum: What difference does difference make?" (1997). *Harvard Educational Review, 67*, 169–187.

Fitzgerald, R., & Fitzgerald, S. (Eds.). (1969). *Flannery O'Connor: Mystery and manners*. New York: Farrar, Straus & Giroux.

Foster, M. (1997). *Black teachers on teaching*. New York: New Press.

Franklin, J. H. (1981). The land of room enough. *Daedalus, 110* (2), 1–12.

Fuentes, C. (1994, Fall). Keynote address at the conference on *The artist in society: Rights, roles, and responsibilities* at the School of the Art Institute of Chicago, Chicago.

Fuqua, P. B. (1994). Teaching, learning, and supervision. In *A decade of progress: Progress in self psychology, Vol. 10* (pp. 79–97). Hillsdale, NJ: Analytic Press.

Gates, H. L., Jr. (1990). Tell me, sir . . . what *is* "black" literature? *Publication of the Modern Language Association of America, 105* (1), 11–22.

Gay, G. (1993). Ethnic minorities and educational equality. In J. A. Banks & C. A. McGee Banks (Eds.), *Multicultural education: Issues and perspectives* (pp. 171–194). Boston: Allyn & Bacon.

Genovese, E. D. (1974). *Roll, Jordan, roll: The world the slaves made*. New York: Pantheon.

Giroux, H. (1987). Schooling and the politics of ethics: Beyond liberal and conservative discourses. *Journal of Education, 169* (2), 9–33.

Gregory, S. S. (1992, March 16). The hidden hurdle. *Time*, pp. 44–46.

Grossman, R., Kirby, J. A., Leroux, C., & Thomas, J. (1994, May 17). Forty years after Brown: Illinois tops list of most segregated. *Chicago Tribune*, pp. 1, 12.

Hacker, A. (1989, October 12). Affirmative action: The new look. *New York Review of Books*, pp. 63–68.

Hacker, A. (1992). *Two nations: Black and white, separate, hostile, unequal*. New York: Scribner.

Hacker, A. (1995). *Two nations: Black and white, separate, hostile, unequal* (expanded and updated). New York: Ballantine.

Henry, W. A., III. (1990, April 9). Beyond the melting pot. *Time*, pp. 28–31.

Hinojosa, R. (1987). *This migrant earth*. Houston: Arte Publico Press.

Hoffman, D. M. (1996). Culture and self in multicultural education: Reflections on discourse, text, and practice. *American Educational Research Journal, 33*, 545–569.

Jacoby, T. (1991, February 18). Psyched out. *The New Republic*, pp. 28–30.

Jones, R. M. (1968). *Fantasy and feeling in education*. New York: New York University Press.

Kleiman, V., & Riggs, M. (Producers), & Riggs, M. (Director). (1991). *Color adjustment* [Video]. San Francisco: California Newsreel.

Kochman, T. (1981). *Black and white styles in conflict*. Chicago: University of Chicago Press.

Lauter, P. (Ed.). (1983). *Reconstructing American literature: Courses, syllabi, issues*. Old Westbury, NY: Feminist Press.

Levine, L. (1993). "Who says?" Learning to value diversity in school. In F. Pignatelli & S. W. Pflaum (Eds.), *Celebrating diverse voices: Progressive education and equity* (pp. 87–111). Newbury Park, CA: Corwin Press, Sage Publications.

Malamud, B. (1983). *The stories of Bernard Malamud*. New York: New American Library.

Malcolm X [Video]. (no date given). Prior Lake, MN: MNTEX.

Martinez-Serros, H. (1988). *The last laugh and other stories*. Houston: Arte Publico Press.

McIntosh, P. (1990). Interactive phases of curricular and personal re-vision with regard to race. Wellesley, MA: Center for Research on Women.

McKeon, R. (Ed.). (1941). *The basic works of Aristotle*. New York: Random House.

Miller, A. (1949). *Death of a salesman*. New York: Viking Press.

Momaday, N. S. (1968). *House made of dawn*. New York: Harper and Row.

Morley, J. (1992). Rap as American history. In L. A. Stanley (Ed.), *Rap the lyrics: The words to rap's greatest hits* (pp. xv–xxxi). New York: Viking Penguin.

Morrison, T. (1973). *Sula*. New York: New American Library.

Morrison, T. (1987). *Beloved*. New York: New American Library.

Morrison, T. (1991, November). Keynote address at *Chicago humanities festival II: Culture contact*, Chicago.

Moses, W. J. (1993). Ambivalent maybe. In G. Early (Ed.), *Lure and loathing: Essays on race, identity, and the ambivalence of assimilation* (pp. 274–290). New York: Allen Lane/Penguin Press.

Navarrette, R. (1993). *A darker shade of crimson*. New York: Bantam.

Naylor, G. (1982). *The women of Brewster Place*. New York: Viking.

Njeri, I. (1993). Sushi and grits: Ethnic identity and conflict in a newly multicultural America. In G. Early (Ed.), *Lure and loathing: Essays on race, identity, and the ambivalence of assimilation* (pp. 13–40). New York: Allen Lane/Penguin Press.

Okazaki, S. (Producer/Director). (1990). *Days of waiting* [Video]. Ho-Ho-Kus, NJ: Mouchette Films.

Omi, M., & Winant, H. (1986). *Racial formation in the United States: From the 1960s to the 1980s.* New York: Routledge and Kegan Paul.

Ozick, C. (1986). The shawl. In S. Cahill (Ed.), *New women and new fiction: Short stories since the sixties* (pp. 2–7). New York: New American Library.

Pack, M. (Producer-Director), & Prizer, J. (Co-Producer). (1993). *Campus culture wars: Five stories about pc* [Video]. Santa Monica, CA: Direct Cinema Ltd.

Pakula, A. J., & Barish, K. (Producers), & Pakula, A. J. (Director). (1982). *Sophie's choice* [Video]. Farmington Hills, MI: CBS/Fox Video.

Paley, V. G. (1989). *White teacher.* Cambridge, MA: Harvard University Press.

Price, R. (1993, February 28). A lifetime of tales from the land of broken hearts [Review of *The collected stories* by William Trevor]. *The New York Times Book Review*, pp. 1, 25–27.

Resnais, A. (Director), & Argos Films (Producer). (1955). *Night and fog* [Video]. Sandy Hook, CT: Video Yesteryear, International Historic Films.

Riggs, M. (Producer/Director). (1987). *Ethnic notions* [Video]. San Francisco: California Newsreel.

Roberts, S. (1993, July 19). Race and politics: Issues that most still sidestep. *The New York Times*, p. B3.

Rodriguez, L. (1993). *Always running: La vida loca: Gang days in L.A.* New York: Touchstone.

Roland, A. (1988). *In search of self in India and Japan: Toward a crosscultural psychology.* Princeton, NJ: Princeton University Press.

Sanchez, S. (1983). Sonia Sanchez. In C. Tate (Ed.), *Black women writers at work* (pp. 132–148). New York: Continuum.

Santayana, G. (1980). *The life of reason: Vol. I. Reason in common sense.* New York: Dover.

Schlesinger, A. M. (1992). *The disuniting of America.* New York: W. W. Norton.

Silko, L. M. (1977). *Ceremony.* New York: Viking Penguin.

Slavin, R. E. (1992). Cooperative learning: Applying contact theory in desegregated schools. In J. Lynch, C. Modgil, & S. Modgil (Eds.), *Cultural diversity and the schools: Vol. II. Prejudice, polemic, or progress?* (pp. 333–348). Bristol, PA: Falmer Press.

Sleeter, C. E., & Grant, C. A. (1987). An analysis of multicultural education in the United States. *Harvard Educational Review, 57,* 421–444.

Smith, A. D. (Director). (1993). *Fires in the mirror* [Video]. Alexandria, VA: PBS Video.

Smith, A. D. (1994). *Twilight: Los Angeles, 1992.* New York: Anchor.

Smith, L. (1949). *Killers of the dream.* New York: W. W. Norton.

Smith, S. (1993, July 18). When terror comes home: Steppenwolf's *Death and the maiden. Chicago Tribune*, Sec. 13, pp. 4, 5, 18.

Spiegelman, A. (1991). *Maus.* New York: Pantheon.

Standiford, L. A. (1982). Worlds made of dawn: Characteristic image and incident in Native American imaginative literature. In H. A. Baker, Jr. (Ed.), *Three American literatures* (pp. 168–196). New York: The Modern Language Association of America.

Steele, S. (1989, February). The recoloring of campus life. *Harper's Magazine*, pp. 47–55.

Steele, S. (1993). I'm black, you're white, who's innocent? In K. Whittemore & G. Marzorati (Eds.), *Voices in black & white: Writings on race in America from Harper's Magazine* (pp. 213–228). New York: Franklin Square Press.

Sternberg, T. (Producer), & Wang, W. (Director). (1989). *Eat a bowl of tea* [Video]. Burbank, CA: RCA/Columbia Pictures Home Video.

Stone, M. (Ed.). (1976). *Between home and community*. Chicago: Francis W. Parker School.

Styron, W. (1979). *Sophie's choice*. New York: Random House.

Suina, J. H. (1991). And then I went to school: Memories of a Pueblo childhood. In *Rethinking Columbus, A Special Edition of Rethinking Schools* (pp. 34–36). Milwaukee: Rethinking Schools Ltd. in collaboration with the Network of Educators on Central America.

Suzuki, B. H. (1989, November/December). Asian Americans as the "model minority" outdoing whites? Or media hype? *Change*, pp. 13–19.

Takaki, R. (1993). *A different mirror*. Boston: Little, Brown.

Tan, A. (1989). *The joy luck club*. New York: Ivy.

Tatge, C., & Lasseur, D. (Directors). (1992). *Bill Moyers: Beyond hate trilogy* [Video]. New York: Mystic Fire Video.

Tatum, B. D. (1992). Talking about race, learning about racism: The application of racial identity development theory in the classroom. *Harvard Educational Review, 62*, 1–24.

Terkel, S. (1992). *Race: How blacks and whites think and feel about the American obsession*. New York: New Press.

Thomas, A. (Producer), & Nava, G. (Director). (1984). *El Norte* [Video]. Farmington Hills, MI: CBS/Fox Video.

Three Rivers, A. (1991). *Cultural etiquette: A guide for the well intentioned*. Indian Valley, VA: Market Wimmin.

Trilling, L. (1965). On the teaching of modern literature. In L. Trilling (Ed.), *Beyond culture: Essays on literature and learning* (pp. 3–30). New York: Viking.

Wacks, J. (Director). (1989). *Powwow highway* [Video]. Beverly Hills, CA: Cannon Video.

Walker, A. (1983). *In search of our mothers' gardens*. New York: Harcourt Brace Jovanovich.

Wehmiller, P. L. (1991, November). Paper presented as part of opening session at the annual conference of the Independent Schools Association of the Central States, Chicago.

Weinberg, T. (Producer). (1991). *The 90s: Vol. 6. Race and racism, red, white, and black* [Video]. Chicago: Subtle Communications.

Weisberg, J. (1991, February 18). Thin skins. *The New Republic*, pp. 22–24.

West, C. (1993). *Race matters*. Boston: Beacon Press.

Wintz, C. D. (1988). *Black culture and the Harlem Renaissance*. Houston: Rice University Press.

Wise, R., & Robbins, J. (Directors). (1997). *West Side Story* [Video version of the 1961 motion picture]. Universal City, CA: MGM/UA Home Video.

Wright, R. (1940). *Native son*. New York: Harper & Row.

INDEX

Adams, M., 77
Addams, Jane, 10, 82
Adler, Mortimer, 105
Adolescence. *See also* High school community
community of peers in, 53–56
identity formation and, 49–53, 58–59
African Americans
as census category, 3
groups for, 20–22, 24, 28
high school Video Club incident, 4–5, 11–13, 25–26, 30–32
intercultural dynamics and, 54–56
Issues of Race and Culture (course), 63, 65–66, 69–71, 76–77, 85–86, 91–92, 94
Jewish Americans and, 54–56, 69–71, 86
school integration and, 1, 61, 101
self-labeling of, 38–39
slavery and, 16, 27, 43, 44, 52–53, 55, 69, 99, 106–107
in student population, ix
writers, 14, 28–29, 33, 34, 35, 40–42, 69–71, 99, 100–101, 102
Afrocentrism, 5
Alienation, 9, 37
Allen, Paula Gunn, 102
American Indians. *See* Native Americans
Andersen, Margaret, 3
Anger, 45–49, 51–52, 65–66
Anson, R. S., 36
Applebee, A. N., 103
Applebome, P., 9, 101
Appleton, Nicholas, 54, 59, 61, 75, 76, 79, 80
Arce, Carlos H., 38, 72
Aristotle, 105
Aronson, E., 75
Ashton-Warner, Sylvia, xi
Asian Americans
as census category, 3

Issues of Race and Culture (course), 63, 71–72, 86
in student population, ix
writers, 33, 71–72, 74, 105–106
Australia, 9

Baker, Houston A., Jr., 34, 41, 43, 85
Baldwin, James, 42, 99, 100, 101
Bambara, Toni Cade, 36
Banks, Cherry A. McGee, x, 43
Banks, James A., ix–xi, x, 35, 43, 46, 74–76, 79, 82
Barish, K., 74
Barnet, S., 69
Beckett, Samuel, 93
Bell, Derrick, 14
Bell, L., 77
Beloved (Morrison), 43, 44, 47, 58, 71, 99, 100
Benson, A., 60, 99, 100
Berman, Paul, 54–55, 61–62, 71
Best Intentions: The Education and Killing of Edmund Perry (Anson), 36
Bigsby, C. W. E., 34, 42
Black and White Styles in Conflict (Kochman), 38
Black Boy (Wright), 103
Blacks. *See* African Americans
Blades, J., 105
Bloom, Allan, 5–6, 33, 83
Blos, Peter, 49, 53
Bourke-White, Margaret, 35
Bridges, Ruby, 1
Brooks, Gwendolyn, 33, 40, 102
Brown v. Board of Education, 61, 101
Burbules, N. C., 79–80
Bureau of the Census, U.S., ix, 3

Caldwell, E., 35
Campos, Pedro Albizu, 72
Carter, S., 28

115

ABOUT THE AUTHOR

Mary Dilg teaches English at the Francis W. Parker School in Chicago. She received the Paul and Kate Farmer Writing Award from the National Council of Teachers of English in 1995 and in 1998.

DATE DUE

SEP 2 5 1999		
MAR 3 0 2000		
8/30/00		
OCT 1 7 2001		
JAN 1 1 2002		
NOV 2 4 2002		
FEB 1 6 2003		
MAR 1 6 2003		
JUN 0 1 2006		
GAYLORD		PRINTED IN U.S.A.